THE NEW INDUSTRIAL SOCIETY

AMERICAN REPUBLIC SERIES

EDITED BY DON E. FEHRENBACHER AND OTIS A. PEASE

THE NEW
INDUSTRIAL
SOCIETY –

BERNARD A. WEISBERGER

John Wiley and Sons, Inc.

NEW YORK · LONDON · SYDNEY · TORONTO

Library of Congress Catalog Card Number: 68-8953
Cloth: SBN 471 92722 8   Paper: SBN 471 92723 6
Printed in the United States of America

Editors' Preface

The Era of Expansion is one of seven volumes in the "Wiley American Republic Series," a joint effort at exploring the meaning of the past to the present. Each of these books is a self-contained study by a specialist in the period treated. Together, they cover the whole chronological range of American history. Designed to be illuminating rather than comprehensive, the Series limits its presentation of factual details in order to make room for fuller explanation of major events and trends. Recognizing, moreover, that the record of the past continually changes as historical data are screened through the minds of different historians, each author in the Series concludes his volume with an extensive historiographical essay, an effective reminder that no one can have the last word on the subject.

Don E. Fehrenbacher
Otis A. Pease

Contents

List of Maps

Maps and charts by John V. Morris

THE NEW INDUSTRIAL SOCIETY

Introduction

The chronicle of human progress from Stone Age to Space Age has been one of change. There is a joke in which the universal father says sagely to Eve as she leaves the Garden of Eden, "My dear, this is an era of transition." Yet, unquestionably, the past hundred years have altered the conditions of human life more swiftly and radically than any preceding century. The metamorphosis has been more stunning in the United States than anywhere else in the world. We passed, almost within a single generation, from self-contained rural isolation to industrial preeminence. Observation of the forces of modernization at work here deepens our understanding of their roots and influence everywhere.

Historians, for a long time, have dealt with the period from the close of Reconstruction in 1877 to the creation of an American overseas empire in 1899 as a separate, definable unit of study. They have tried to condense its essence into a handful of words, calling it the age of industrialization, urbanization, concentration, organization, or expansion. The era eludes these easy brands. Instead of beginning with generalization and sinking into detail it is more revealing to reverse the process and simply try to determine what there was about the United States of 1900 that made it a visibly different country from what it had been a generation earlier.

The face of the land was significantly changed. In the Far West, steel rails shimmered in the deserts or clung to the cliffsides once known only to trappers' eyes. In the East, too, the locomotive whistle's whoop filled once-quiet valleys and denoted the time of day in every hamlet. The railroad was a novelty in 1846 and an accomplishment in 1876. By the end of the century it was the indispensable and omnipresent element of national growth and cohesion.

1

By 1900, much of the continent beyond the Mississippi River still deserved the name "wide open spaces." However, across thousands of square miles, silos and windmills pointed to the sky; barbed-wire fences defined property and the advance of law; and farmers, in harvesting machines, thrashed like insects through the wheatfields. Where buffalo trails, wheel ruts of traders' wagons, and Indian ponies' hoofmarks once intersected at fords, rail junctions now stood, marked by warehouses and grain elevators. Barns and ranch houses gleamed in fresh paint where cowboys had gazed across emptiness at the horizon. Towns like Denver and Butte, still shaggy and raw in 1876, now included smelting works, banks, offices, hotels, miners' shacks, and million-aires' mansions. The banks and smelters often featured on their signboards the names of Eastern corporations.

The South, too, was different. A passenger of 1900, riding along its thousands of miles of new rail lines, would have seen striking contrasts with the countryside of 1860 and even of 1876. On former plantations, peeling hovels housed ragged sharecroppers—black and white—who plodded behind their mules to the cotton fields. Although there were still hundreds of crossroad towns where loafers whittled in front of the courthouse as they had done in steamboat days, there were new things to see, too. There were new factories and businesses in New Orleans, Memphis, Nashville, and Atlanta. There were textile mills and yellow frame company houses in the Piedmont region of the Carolinas. There were steel mills in Birmingham and lumber camps in the pine woods of Arkansas, Louisiana, and Florida.

In the northeastern quarter of the nation—amid the rocks of Pilgrim New England, the gentle countryside of western New York, the shadowed clefts of the Appalachians, and the once-forested stretches of the Old Northwest—there was scarcely a few hour's ride that did not bring a traveler to some city where smoke, steel, and flame mingled day and night. He beheld the industrial heartland of America—a continuous scene of shrieking factories, roaring furnaces, clashing railyards, and thick-clustered humanity.

The occupations and living habits of the Americans who populated the transformed land had also changed. Millions more of them lived in cities that exceeded fifty thousand than had been the case in 1875, and they enjoyed the luxury of telephones, electric lights, elevators, and street railways—none of which were in existence on the hundredth birthday of independence.

An American boy under sixteen in 1900 was more likely to be in school than his father had been at the same age. An American woman, especially if unmarried, was more likely than her mother to be working. Her job depended greatly on her family background. Workingmen's daughters were drawn into the factory or domestic service. A girl whose parents could afford to let her attend high school had brighter prospects. By acquiring attainments such as manners, diction, and a grasp of business arithmetic, she might become a salesgirl or join the swelling ranks of female office workers. If her aims were even higher, and support beyond high school was available, she could go on to a "normal school" and become a teacher. Girls from well-off families were increasingly inclined to continue to higher education, either at the state university or at one of the many new women's colleges. There, a few of them prepared for professions, and most of them equipped themselves to transmit culture to scientifically raised husbands and children. Whatever her status, the American woman of 1900 was encouraged to look toward wider horizons than her grandmother had known.

The span of two and a half decades also did much to alter the terms on which Americans earned their bread. The typical industrial worker in almost any field in 1900 operated more complex, costly, and productive machines than those that had seemed so marvelous at the Centennial Exposition of 1876. If he was one of the fifteen percent of workers who belonged to a labor union, it was probably affiliated with the American Federation of Labor, which was not formed until 1886. The American who derived his income from a profession was more likely than ever to be college-trained. If he practiced medicine or was in any scientific field, his work was affected by discoveries and developments in the graduate schools of the great universities which, for the most part, did not exist in 1876. If he was self-employed as a businessman, he was dealing in goods that were mass-produced by a shrinking number of independent firms, with prices set by national combinations of capitalists. Finally, the American farmer at the end of the century very probably owned, or was indebted for, machinery whose total value exceeded that of his land and buildings. He was a more productive and well-informed agriculturalist than his father, and probably was better clothed and housed, but he was also less likely to be a part-time minister or professional man or to achieve public office.

The very meaning of the phrase "the American people" had been renewed since 1876. By 1900 the term embraced a population diversified by millions of recent arrivals from eastern Europe and Asia. True, hopeful Englishmen, Germans, Scots, Irishmen, Frenchmen, and Dutchmen had sought American shores as early as colonial times; by the 1870s immigration itself was no novelty. But the nations which, after 1890, furnished "new" Americans were not familiar lands. Poles, Russians, Bohemians, Serbs, Hungarians, Italians, Armenians, Syrians, Greeks, and Finns appeared on the passenger lists of arriving steamers. The total number of arrivals from these eastern and southern European countries increased until it exceeded the number arriving from Scandinavia, Germany, and the British Isles. Chinese and Japanese were already numerous on the West Coast and, under political pressure from California, the federal government barred further immigration from China in 1882.

The new immigrants were no more numerous in proportion to the whole populace than the old immigrants had been in earlier days. But they were poor, unacclimated, and often were concentrated in the cities. A thousand Swedes, scattered across the emptiness of a Dakota prairie county, created no uneasiness among American neighbors in 1900, nor did the by-then-familiar faces of Irish or German workers, storekeepers, and policemen. But rural-born, Protestant Americans, who sat on streetcars full of dark-featured Italians on the way to factories, or walked through crowded streets where fierce, ragged men clamored in a dozen tongues and bearded figures in strange garb hurried toward synagogues or Catholic chapels, were possessed by a sense that they themselves—the "original" citizenry of the United States—were living in another country.

There were also new styles in national leadership a quarter of a century after Grant left the White House. The generation of the so-called robber barons had then marveled at the careers of Vanderbilt, Armour, Huntington, Gould, Guggenheim, Morgan, Rockefeller, McCormick, Carnegie, and many others. In 1900 many of these business leaders were still actively managing their own enterprises; some of them had retired to their ornate mansions; others traveled in search of culture and worthy sons-in-law; and a few pursued political ambitions. Rockefeller and Carnegie, in particular, were establishing a new pattern, as bold as any they had designed for their industries. Both of them retired from business and began long, intensely active careers as philanthropists on a huge scale. Eventually these activities would change the image of the rich man. He would become identified with the universities and institutions founded by his fortunes, his children would often seek public service, and his economic empire would be administered by directors whose own identities were merged in the identity of the company. Individualism in corporate leadership was on the decline, and similar trends were evident in other fields as diverse as journalism and revivalism.

In politics the Presidency had declined in symbolic majesty under Grant,

Hayes, Garfield, Arthur, and Benjamin Harrison. Cleveland had restored some strength to the office and, in 1900, McKinley was highly popular, but no really inspiring spokesman of national purpose had occupied the White House for thirty-five years. Nor had the postwar Senate produced any statesman to rank with the giants of the young republic like Clay, Calhoun, Benton, or Webster.

Yet important political changes were taking place as the twentieth century opened. However, they were not always widely apparent because their full influence would develop much later—like the impact of pioneering scientific work in 1900 in the areas of radio waves, automobiles, and airplanes. On the surface, politics seemed to be what it had been in 1877, a game with familiar rules and players. The opponents were Republicans and Democrats, state governments and the federal government, East and West, North and South, farmer and manufacturer. The two major parties emerged from the 1890s stronger than ever. They were still broadly based, and they had fought off the effort of the Populists to break two-party dominance of elections.

But these traditional antagonisms of political life were in the process of modification. The defeat of Populism proved, among other things, that it was impossible to mobilize the nation's farmers under one banner. The interests of agriculture and industry could not be easily separated in a complex social order. Moreover, the federal-state conflict was declining in intensity as Washington steadily enlarged the scope of its powers. In 1887 the national government tentatively moved into the sphere of economic regulation through the creation of the Interstate Commerce Commission, an initially weak agency, but the forerunner of many more to come. In 1890 Congress enacted an antitrust act which, although vague and unimplemented, was nonetheless a pathbreaking statement of federal intention to administer justice in the business world. And in 1900 the federal government was displaying its power and reach in the management of new overseas possessions. This was an extension of its historical role in administering the public domain, which called for much greater sophistication and expenditure.

The machinery through which national power was exerted was itself modernized. The Federal Civil Service Act of 1883 was more than a blow at political office seeking. It cleared the ground for securing professional staffs for the bureaus and agencies of Washington. Congress also was changing its own pattern of operation. Much of its work was conducted in committees and in informal gatherings of party leaders. In the House of Representatives, especially, strict procedural rules limited the subjects and lengths of debate.

Consequently, since many issues were decided off the floor, there was a decline in both the need and appreciation for congressional oratory. But the new system enabled an enlarged legislative branch to dispose of many and various items of business.

Meanwhile the Supreme Court played its own role in transforming the relationships between the states and the nation by a series of decisions that curbed the powers of the state legislatures with regard to the regulation of railroads and other corporations. These decisions were not limited to a restriction of the states; often they were intended to exert a check on the federal government as well. Therefore, the justices who rendered them were not, like John Marshall, articulate spokesmen of national purpose and power. Instead, they were judicial conservatives erecting protective walls around business.

The waning of genuine antagonism between the North and the South was another striking sign of a changed political order. In 1876 the passions of wartime and Reconstruction still heavily influenced voting behavior. In 1900 Southerners continued to pay cultural reverence to the Confederate era, but investments of Northern capital in Dixieland created new issues that cut across geographic boundaries. Votes in Congress followed cleavages of economic interest rather than dividing lines between the Blue and the Gray. Throughout the nation, popular literature sentimentalized the entire war in a fashion acceptable to the veterans who were mellowing into their sixties. In hindsight, almost everyone in the uniform of either side was principled and valorous.

The American Negro, however, was a victim of this fraternization. In 1876 the country had completed an eleven-year experiment in social change during which the victorious North had freed the slave, had clothed him with constitutional guarantees of equal citizenship, and had given him the ballot. By 1900 the civil rights of Negroes were overwhelmed in a rising tide of white supremacy—legally enforced in the Southern states (but unofficially endorsed by the entire nation) and left intact by the Supreme Court. More than twenty years of post-Reconstruction "progress" had made the United States a less promising place for nonwhites (including Indians and Orientals) than it had been just after the Civil War.

The trend of political development in 1900 was steadily away from parochial concerns. An illustration was in the steady increase of the public's concern with the ills of the city. Reform magazines speculated anxiously whether "bossism" could be overthrown and whether the gargantuan problems of the metropolis could be solved by governmental innovation. For each major urban community, these were "local" problems, but the rising nationwide number of big cities, whose difficulties were generally similar, made "the city" a subject of national attention. The enlarged city, like the enlarged corporation, was a force that dictated new political issues and alignments.

Voting allegiances were determined by men's reactions to the conflict between private management and public interest arising in a variety of new settings. A machine-ridden city was one setting; a strike-bound railroad system was another; depleted forests and grazing lands were still another. Although states and sections sometimes became involved in these struggles, the basic emotional loyalties to the states and sections that had shaped American politics for the first century under the Constitution were diminished. A "new nationalism" had been born long before it became the name of Theodore Roosevelt's political program in 1910.

The historian who studies these changes must arrive at a definition before he weighs their meaning. Did they, taken together, create a "new" America? The question can best be answered by first examining some of the characteristic institutions and beliefs of the "old" republic. The profiles of American society in 1875 and 1900 must be compared to determine whether they are distinctly different.

The American of the 1870s believed, as firmly as his father, in individualism and competition as the spurs to what Lincoln once called "laudable ambition." He expected to find a calling, to prosper in it, and to rise in status as his property and family matched each other in growth. He was an entrant in the race of life and was conditioned to making a hard run of it.

If he forged ahead, however, it was not necessarily at his neighbor's expense. Softening the harsh edge of the doctrine of competition, there was faith in the abundance of opportunity. Free land seemed always available for the taking. A man of spirit, it was believed, could go West and grow up with the country. Past experience indicated that a freeborn American could quickly pick up the rudiments of law or medicine. Also, with equal ease, he could open a store, a mill, a transportation line, a university, or a state government complete with a constitution. A single failure was merely a cue for a fresh effort elsewhere.

The individualistic American of Grant's day, however, did not lack practice in community participation. The society most familiar to him was that of the village or small town. Far more than the open frontier or the few great cities, it tested the capacity of Americans for sharing responsibilities. Editors, lawyers, politicians, businessmen, and educators practiced their skills and children learned their expected roles in the dust of Main Street. The town was homogeneous. Its people were generally Protestant, white, literate (but not addicted to reading for pleasure), industrious, and practical. There were few foreigners, millionaires, or paupers in small-town America. On Sundays almost everyone attended Methodist, Baptist, or Presbyterian church services. The minister not only led in prayer but encouraged the work of the local chapters of the Temperence Society, the Missionary Society, and other elements in the network of national associations that bound villages together and convinced congregations that their social patterns were indistinguishable from God's will and the national purpose.

Two great articles of faith united most Americans who were grown men and women by 1875. One was an overwhelming sense of America's moral superiority as evidenced in its political institutions; that is, a confidence that national success registered divine approval of the United States' plan of government. The other was the belief in democracy. No one failed to realize that there were distinctions of intellect, wealth, and achievement among individuals, but almost everyone affirmed the basic equality of all men "before the law" and the value of submitting controversial issues to the judgment of the sovereign electorate. Certain classes were excepted from the faith in popular wisdom—notably women, Negroes, children, lunatics, and criminals. Nevertheless, democracy was more than a hollow shrine before which America worshipped.

The energies generated by these beliefs and customs had built the country. The effect that rapid industrial growth had on these beliefs and customs is one of the truest barometers of social change in an era of growth.

The large-scale organization of economic activity savagely undercut both the myth and the reality of a nation of freely competing individuals. Few lone entrepreneurs could aspire to the ownership of major productive elements in a mass-production economy that kept its accounts in millions. The consolidation of business organizations bound together all operators in a network of dependency. Major economic decisions in the new order were not made by the impersonal forces of competition but were made by people who held power in the largest corporation and bank headquarters. Limits to this power could not be imposed by individuals. Only counter-organization was effective. Unions, granges, and other pressure groups were no longer simple fraternal and self-help associations but became combat units in economic warfare.

The country was still rich in opportunities, but the opportunities were different from those celebrated by Lincoln. A farmer could not easily find free land. The public domain was far from exhausted, even in 1900, but high-quality farms close to transportation routes were not readily available, and the initial capital investment to work them successfully was prohibitive. The would-be yeoman had to begin his career in partnership with the bank.

The expansion of business created innumerable new openings for salesmen, technicians, and managers. But persons who climbed the ladder of social mobility within corporation ranks remained salaried employees and were not truly independent or self-made. A growing population needed more professional men, but the achievement of that status became more difficult. Society was undoubtedly the gainer from heightened standards of competence in law, medicine, engineering, and teaching. One result, however, was to end self-tutoring or apprenticeship as a mode of preparation for those callings. Now the pursuit of a profession was open only to people who had the means to travel the demanding road to higher education.

The hamlet suffered most from technological progress. It became a tributary of the nearest great city, which drained away its brightest and best young blood. The metropolis offered enormous cultural advantages over the town and, by its very existence, illustrated the immense potentialities of applied engineering and organization. Yet the overshadowing by the metropolis of its smaller neighbors destroyed them as self-contained communities, confident of their ability to deal equitably with any problems.

These changes might have been expected to shake the ancient faith of Americans in their country's bright future and in their own powers of self-rule. But they did not have such a melancholy result. Individualism, equal opportunity, and self-sufficient communities might undergo deep alterations, but belief in American destiny and the virtues of democracy persisted. Official spokesmen for the national viewpoint in 1900 praised the achievements of these Americans who had built the modern United States. These spokesmen considered its power and wealth to be surer signs than ever of divine favor. Some speakers replaced God as the source of blessings with Progress, But the import of their message was the same. Only a few dissenting voices, like those of two grandsons of John Quincy Adams—Henry and Brooks—questioned the shape of the future. They were not widely heeded.

The American people had not lost their confidence in the assumptions of free government in the years from Hayes' election to McKinely's reelection. They had learned that the mere existence of democratic machinery did not guarantee liberty; they had seen corporations buy votes in state and municipal legislatures and make hired men of governors and judges; they had seen the poor sometimes rendered unequal before the law in contests with wealth and influence. Yet they remained convinced, for the most part, that the electorate, if informed and aroused, could cope with these problems. They did not demand a Caesar, or an aristocracy of talent (or of any other kind), or socialism, or anarchism to save them. When they dealt politically with the problems of the new age, it was by extending instead of restricting the scope of their elected servants' powers. Under the impact of industrialism, democratic practice had to be widely revised but, as a faith and a standard, democracy survived well.

The observer who moves to a final high level of generalization notices that the American people, between 1875 and 1900, underwent adjustments that were part of the experience of all mankind. Modern civilization and science opened tremendous new sources of power that could be applied to productive ends. With the strength and speed of steam and electricity behind them, the forces of industrial development swept over the globe, seeking raw materials, markets, and workers. Old forms of social organization and belief toppled before the demands of the machine. Religions, family patterns, traditions, laws, and local governments were shaken and broken in Scotland, Germany, Hungary, the Congo, and Indochina—almost everywhere in the world—as much as in rural Illinois and Maine.

The meaning of United States history was interwoven with the meaning of all modern history. Machine-age man has entered a realm where his powers of self-improvement and self-obliteration are hugely magnified and delicately balanced. In the last quarter of the nineteenth century, Americans—unconscious of these frightening implications—achieved their first deep penetration of this realm.

Chapter II

The Reorganization of the American Economy, 1850 to 1901

Come, Muse, migrate from Greece and Ionia
. . . .
For know a better, fresher, busier sphere, a wide, untried domain awaits, demands
    you.
. . . .
Steam-power, the great express lines, gas, petroleum.
These triumphs of our time, the Atlantic's delicate cable,
The Pacific railroad, the Suez Canal, the Mont Cenis and Gothard and Hoosac
    tunnels, the Brooklyn Bridge,
This earth all spann'd with iron rails, with lines of steamship threadings every sea,
Our own rondure, the current globe I bring.

Walt Whitman, *Song of the Exposition* (of 1876)

Thus, Walt Whitman invoked the muse of a new era. Although defenders of poetic convention might have found these lines startling, engineers, bankers, and statisticians could understand the inspiration of the nineteenth century's incredible industrial growth. As the economist David A. Wells stated in 1889:

"Within the preceding thirty years, man in general has attained to such a greater control over the forces of Nature, and has so compassed their use, that he has been able to do far more work in a given time, produce far more product, measured by quantity in ratio to a given amount of labor, and reduce the effort necessary to insure a comfortable subsistence in a far greater measure [than had ever before been possible]."

11

What Wells called "an almost total revolution" had transformed every branch of industry.

This revolution is the dominating theme of modern American history and world history. In the United States its impact was swift, powerful, and all-encompassing. It created a new nation.

TECHNOLOGY IN TRIUMPH

Traditional accounts of American industrial growth begin with the ending of the Civil War, but it is a mistake to trace economic growth by essentially political milestones. By economic measure, the industrialization of American life began long before 1865. Railroad construction, bank loans, the value added to raw materials by manufacture, immigration, the size of investments in agricultural and other machinery, and production of certain key commodities such as pig iron and bituminous coal had increased by as much as two hundred percent between 1840 and 1860. An important current economic theorist, Walt W. Rostow, has even asserted that the American "takeoff" into sustained, modern, dominating economic growth was completed by 1860, and what took place thereafter was a flight to maturity. In fact, the 1860s show an uneven pattern of growth in the production of goods considered essential to "industrialism," which is understandable in the light of the war. Naturally cotton production decreased. The annual mileage of newly built railroad line dropped quite sharply from over 3400 in 1854 to only 574 in 1863, and did not exceed the 1854 level until 1869. There was no spectacular increase in the rate of growth of sales of agricultural implements. Production of iron and coal trended upward, but with no sharp wartime spurt. One distinguished economic historian has even argued that the war retarded industrialization by concentrating productive efforts on short-run military needs. This view has been challenged, however, and the argument seems to turn on *which* indices of production are evidences of "industrialization," and on the length of the periods over which growth or decline should be measured. Whoever is right, the unqualified assertion that the Civil War "hastened" industrialism can no longer be made safely.

Nevertheless, there is no doubt that the postwar rate of climb was swift. Railroad mileage, for example, which stood at approximately 35,000 in 1865, doubled in the next eight years, passed the hundred thousand mark in 1881, and by 1900 had very nearly doubled even this figure, reaching a total of 193,000 miles at the end of the century. The national rail net mileage reached its maximum with 254,000 miles of track in 1916. Construction of new line reached a yearly high of nearly 13,000 miles in 1887. Although the most spectacular building feats were in the Far West, where five transcontinental lines were stretched across desert and mountain, there was more economic meaning in the growth of the feeder lines in older sections. Industrial growth thrived on a truly national market, which saw Chicago harvesters, Texas beef, Minneapolis flour, Waterbury clocks, and Toledo glass rushed to almost any populated place on the map at thirty or more miles an hour. Railroad growth also stoked the fires of the steel mills, the second great element in modern industrial power. As the builders cried out for the tough new metal after 1865 (to replace older, cast-iron rails in addition to laying new track, much as modern airlines converted to jet operation), there was an escalation of demand that spurred investment, modernization, and prodigies of production in a steel industry which had scarcely existed until the discovery of the Bessemer process just before the Civil War began. Steel was also wanted for bridges, machinery, wire, armorplate, and construction work, and it was not unnatural that the total of American-produced steel ingots and castings should rise from less than 20,000 long tons in 1867 to a world-leading ten million long tons in 1900.

The consumption of energy other than that provided by human and animal muscle rose steadily. Bituminous coal production increased from about 13 million short tons in 1867 to 212,316,000 short tons in 1900. In 1860 there was no such thing as an American petroleum products industry; by 1899 more than 1 billion gallons of kerosene, 300 million gallons of fuel oils, and 170 million gallons of lubricating oils were manufactured. This took place before the gasoline engine created its own revolution in demand. Electricity as a source of both light and power became a practical reality in the 1880s but, by 1912, industry alone was using more than 11 million kilowatt hours in a single year. Central generating plants, to provide illumination and street railway transportation for entire cities, were commonplace. The total horsepower for doing basic industrial work produced from all sources—steam, electricity, wind, water, and work animals—was approximately 2,535,000 in 1860 and 46,215,000 in 1900. This was nearly an 18-fold increase in energy applicable to production in one lifetime. Small wonder that Henry Adams declared in 1904 in a prophetic image: "Power leaped from every atom. . . Man could no longer hold it off. Forces grasped his wrists and flung him about as though he had hold of a live wire."

Year after year the nation's factories poured out capital goods such as

The huge Corliss engines furnishing the power for the exhibits at the Centennial Exposition were tangible signs of the industrial strength that the United States would display in her second century of independence.

The American exhibit at London's Crystal Palace Exposition of 1850 showed America's then-embryonic industry at work. The farm implements and revolvers vied for attention with such art works as "The Dying Indian" and Hiram Powers' unclad "Greek Slave" (not shown). Contrast this with the picture of the Chicago Fair forty-three years later, when an entire building was needed to show the electrical exhibits alone.

agricultural, mining and construction machinery, locomotives, generators, chemicals, and such consumer items as flour, fabrics, canned foods, clothing, boots and shoes, furniture, lamps, cutlery, stoves, wagons, hardware, paints, lacquers, paper and printing presses, cigars, and sewing machines. In a generation the country moved from a homemade to a store-bought society. And this revolutionary transformation was achieved by technical change that enabled mass production to bring an infinite variety of goods within the reach of every man's purse. Andrew Carnegie wrote exultantly

The huge and brilliantly illuminated Electricity Building at the Chicago World's Fair of 1893 was a somewhat ornate temple to the power of the dynamo which Henry Adams saw as one of the deities of the incoming century.

that with steel billets selling at $15 a gross ton, the consumer got 1 pound of steel for two thirds of 1 cent. Into this pound went 2 pounds of iron ore, mined and transported 1000 miles, $1\frac{1}{3}$ pounds of coal mined, roasted into coke, and carried 50 miles, and $\frac{1}{3}$ pound of limestone quarried and transported 140 miles. Carnegie gave primary credit for this incredible cheapening of cost to automatic machinery.

Actually there were few industries in which mechanization did not work magic. The publicized inventions that come readily to mind—the telephone, the typewriter, the electric light, all dating from the 1870s—were but the peak of the iceberg. There were also innumerable significant but little-known industrial innovations. Consider two examples. In glassmaking, during the years between 1880 and 1916, machines were developed that automatically blew and shaped bulbs, tumblers, lamp chimneys, and bottles. Machines were developed that automatically produced glass tubing and rods of uniform thickness for any purpose. Other machines automatically rolled out continuous sheets of window glass between rollers as rapidly as five feet (of seven-foot wide glass) per minute. Moreover, there were improvements in furnaces, fuels, and additives to molten glass, which improved quality as well as quantity. Between 1880 and 1919, the number of firms making glass jumped from 169 to 317. The number of workers involved increased from 24,000 to 83,600. But the physical volume of the glass produced increased 10-fold, and the value of the glass produced increased more than 12-fold—from approximately $21 million in 1880 to $261,884,080 in 1919. Or consider the daily newspaper. In 1840, a good-sized "big-city" newspaper consisted of 4 or 6 pages, was sold to perhaps 4000 subscribers daily, and cost between 5 and 10 cents. In the ensuing 50 years, machines were developed that printed both sides of a continuous sheet of paper and automatically cut and folded finished pages, while other machines set type mechanically. By 1890, as a result of work such as that of the Hoe Company in press technology or Ottmar Mergenthaler, developer of the linotype, a major New York newspaper such as the *New York World* reached perhaps 300,000 people daily with an edition of 16 or more pages, for 2 cents. By the end of the century, the newspapers were even larger—and Sunday editions contained colored supplements, photographs, and other attractions in as many as 64 pages of wood-pulp paper (itself a post-Civil War development).

It was in lowly personifications such as the throw-away beer bottle and the colored comics that the miracle of productivity revealed itself to many Americans who never saw a blast furnace or a dynamo. But whatever shape technological triumph took, it was the dominating cultural, social, intellectual, and political fact of the age.

THE ORGANIZATION OF ABUNDANCE

Changes such as these brought on sweeping reorganizations of the system by which business in the United States was managed. The paradox of mass production was that it produced items for pennies through the use of machines and a transportation network costing hundreds of millions of dollars. These monster complexes demanded strong centralized control. The wasteful duplication inherent in free competition became a heavy burden on persons who produced on a large scale. In the "game of business," it was necessary each year for a player to put up higher and higher stakes to stay at the table, and this led to a further paradox. Small players had to drop out, and the nation could not afford to lose many really big players, since they took too many investors and employees down with them. Hence, to some extent, the game had to be rigged.

A revealing sign of the trend toward bigness and combination was the rise of the corporation. The partnership, which was the favored form of combining capital in colonial times, had serious drawbacks for large-scale enterprise. It was vulnerable to deaths, arguments among partners, and individual failures, and could not amass the really great sums of capital demanded by modernized industry.

In the corporation, by contrast, shares of stock could be sold in enormous quantities. Shareholders were able to sell or transfer their holdings freely and to elect directors who, through appointed professional managers, could conduct the business. An individual shareholder could only lose the value of his own shares in case of trouble. Thus, directors might come and go, shareholders might die and sell out, but the corporation went on undisturbed, raising and spending millions. These qualities of durability and bigness explain the growing popularity of corporate organization, especially in fields such as banking, canal building, and railroading, during the early phases of economic growth, when the need for large outlays over long periods became apparent. New York's Erie Railroad, for example, was begun in 1833 with an estimated construction cost of three million dollars. By the time it was completed from Lake Erie to the mouth of the Hudson, in 1851, its actual expense had exceeded fifty million dollars.

Corporation charters originally had been granted only by special acts of the state legislature to individual applicants but, during the 1840s, Jacksonian Democrats in industrial states succeeded in replacing this system with general incorporation laws, which allowed any group, on payment of a fee, to create a company and sell stock. The path was thus open for widespread use of this organizational device, which was so well suited to the new age of big business. Data for early corporations are not available, but the triumph of the system is revealed by figures which show that, in 1904, almost seventy percent of all manufacturing employees were in corporation-owned establishments.

But there was a price for this growth. The corporations themselves, grown to monstrous size, became "privileged members of society." The Southern Pacific Railroad, for instance, with a virtual monopoly of rail transport in California and limitless funds to hire lawyers, lobbyists, and editors, dominated the life of that state for two decades after 1880. To the bigness of the corporations there was joined an impersonality summed up in the popular phrase that a corporate entity had neither a soul to be damned nor a body to be kicked. Moreover, there was another problem connected with the system—a problem that arose because shares of stock could be bought, sold, and swapped on the open market, for profit, by men who had no interest in the fate of the businesses represented by the stock certificates.

A kind of elegant gambling took place, involving two types of transactions known as "buying long" and "selling short." A contract was made to buy or sell stocks for a set price on some future date. If the price had risen at the appointed time, the buyer profited: he got stocks at less than the going rate. If the price had fallen, the seller got more than the market figure for the shares he unloaded. The trouble with this simple wager was that the speculative buyers (or "bulls") and sellers (known as "bears") did not leave the price to chance. Bulls often made heavy secret purchases in order to bid up prices temporarily and artificially. Bears were not above buying control of a company and then issuing shares of stock far in excess of the value of its properties (a process known as "watering the stock"), finally dumping the shares on the market to drive prices down. Other forms of knavery were possible through manipulation of the securities market. Unethical majority stockholders (and the directors whom they controlled) could use a company's assets to support loans, expansion, or construction that was economically unsound but that promised immediate profits to persons on the inside. A master of this kind of manipulation was Jay Gould.

He was once a store clerk and tannery operator who, in the 1880s, became a multimillionaire owner of half the rail lines in the Southwest. He also owned a newspaper, the New York City elevated railway system, and the Western Union telegraph company without any evident knowledge of (or interest in) journalism or transportation.

Rascality, on a grand scale, was not typical of the American business system, but it had painful consequences. Companies—railroads, in particular—were left with enormous debts, based not on the companies' actual earning power but on the false paper value of their watered stocks. Even worse, the wild fluctuations in stock prices involved the banks, which lived by investing other people's money in securities. When a sudden fall in the market wiped out a bank or banks, business loans were called in, factory doors closed, goods could find no buyers at any price, and the whole nation lurched into a sickening depression. In 1873, the failure of a major banking house triggered a paralyzing four-year slump. It was a national lesson in the complexity and the interdependence of the new economic system. It was also evidence of the dangers in a pattern of corporate financing which often divorced the ownership of an enterprise from responsibility for its management.

Yet the corporations, socially troublesome as they were, checked each others' power through competition, where it existed. The genuine problems of the age of big business emerged more starkly when individual firms, bled by price wars and the costs of modernization, forsook competition and combined. Once again certain railroads—pioneers of American industrial development—took a pace-setting role in the 1870s by setting up "pools." These pools were arrangements whereby allegedly competing lines divided traffic among themselves, and then shared earnings periodically on a prorated basis. An example was the so-called "Iowa Pool" of 1870, in which three lines running between Chicago and Omaha shared equally the heavy grain and livestock shipments of the route. Another example was the South Improvement Company. It was an organization of oil refiners and directors of the New York Central, the Erie, and the Pennsylvania railroads that aimed at dividing the oil-carriage business between Cleveland and the Atlantic Coast. The Pennsylvania railroad was to get 45 percent of the traffic, and the other two lines were to divide the balance evenly. In order to encourage the shippers to go along with this practice of "evening" the shipments, they were given rebates on the published rates—and, as an added advantage, rebates on the shipments of their competitors! In theory, these were merely rewards for allowing the railroads to save money by efficient planning but, in fact, the rebates allowed the "eveners" to ruin their competitors. The railroads, therefore, by giving up competition themselves, were enabling certain shippers to dominate their own industries. Public outcry against this abuse of the railroads' role as "common carriers" soon forced an end to the South Improvement Company. Yet pools not only continued to exist among railroads but also were organized in the coal, iron, and other industries. Production quotas were allotted, and prices were set. The consumer lost the benefit of prices lowered by competition, although it has been argued that he also got the benefit of an industry that could improve itself by planning ahead with certainty. The thorny question remained, however: How could some public control be exerted over the policies of the "planners"?

The pool, as a device for combination, had a drawback. It enjoyed no legal standing, and therefore its ground rules could not be enforced in court. In 1882, a new instrument was invented that added an unforgettable word to American history—the "trust." The first modern industrial trust was created by one of the refining firms involved in the South Improvement Company: Standard Oil of Ohio. The stockholders in Standard Oil turned over their properties to the management of a board of "trustees," chosen from among themselves. The trustees could also hold the stocks of other oil-producing, marketing, and refining corporations under the same agreement. Thus a large number of companies in the same business, while retaining their individual identity under various state laws and appearing to be freely competing firms, could actually be operated as a single business.

Standard Oil was so extraordinarily successful—by 1898 it refined 83.7 percent of the oil in the United States—that it became the symbol for concentration, and "trust" became a synonym for any dominating concern or group of concerns in an industry (even where the formal device of trusteeship was not used). The Standard Oil corporation was the creation of a mild-looking, pious, Cleveland businessman named John D. Rockefeller, who entered the oil industry on a full-time basis in 1865. By a brilliant combination of long-range planning, exacting cost accountancy, occasional gambles, and unhesitating use of economic power, he brought stability to the business of drilling, pumping, processing, and selling oil—a venture so risky at first that its symbol was the wildcat.

The story of Standard Oil's rise to the top defies compression into a few paragraphs, but the significant thing about it was how well it showed the two sides of the coin of concentration. At the time of Rockefeller's greatest power, the nation enjoyed the modern marvel of an oil business capable of supplying plentiful, regular, and cheap quantities of lubricants and illuminants to any spot on the globe that was civilized enough to use them. Yet Standard's dominance of every aspect of oil transactions (from hole-in-the-ground to customer) made a joke out of the cherished myth that American economic life offered opportunity to all through free competition. When critics of the new social order looked for horrible examples, Standard Oil's name led all the rest.

But it was only one of many. The advantages of combination were irresistible and, by the late 1890s, combinations of producers were achieving productive prodigies but were squeezing the life out of competition in many diverse fields—iron and steel, whiskey, cordage, biscuits, matches, lead, sugar, and cottonseed oil. The formal "trust" device itself was replaced by another legal entity—the holding company—a single firm that held controlling blocks of the stock of other firms. As one historian notes, this "signalized the final triumph of the corporation, for now corporations could be made to combine corporations." After 1890, holding companies, or outright mergers, became even more conspicuous on the industrial scene. A landmark in size was reached in 1901, when United States Steel was formed, merging 158 companies involved in steelmaking into a single organization capitalized at nearly one and one-half billion dollars. The number of major combinations rose from 12 to 305 between 1897 and 1903, despite clamors of alarm (to be discussed later) concerning the political and social effects of such monstrous aggregations of wealth. "You might as well endeavor to stay the formation of clouds, the falling of the rains, or the flowing of the streams, as to attempt . . . to prevent organization of industry," observed Rockefeller's counsel, S.T.C. Dodd, with considerable satisfaction. Fifty years after the end of the Civil War, names such as Standard Oil, U.S. Steel, General Electric, American Telephone and Telegraph, and American Tobacco were already symbols of a new strength that controlled the lion's share of manufacturing in the United States.

NEW PATTERNS OF LEADERSHIP

A portentous side effect of the new gigantism in industrial organization was the emergence of the "big businessman" as a social model and hero. Wealth had always bred social and political power. A William Byrd of colonial Virginia, a John Hancock of Revolutionary Massachusetts, a John

Jacob Astor of the republic's early days, all bestrode their local communities self-confidently, knowing that their lands, ships, storehouses, and trading posts made them men of might. The thrust of "Jacksonian democracy," in fact, had been toward reducing the frankly asserted privileges of the already rich, and toward opening the avenues of affluence to new blood.

But the post-Civil war corporation heads were something new. They were no longer simply rich men, enjoying the fruits of traffic in goods and lands. They controlled the indispensable tools of the new economy. As railroad owners they dominated the arteries of the nation. As manufacturers they set the prices of things absolutely indispensable to modern existence—power and the coal to produce it; bread for the industrial worker; farm machinery to harvest the wheat for the bread; and steel to make the farm machinery. As bankers they dealt in millions and hundreds of millions of dollars, and when they made a mistake, every business establishment in the country was likely to rock because of it. It was no wonder that their generation thought of them as towering figures, whether denouncing them as "monopolists" or hailing them as "captains of industry." Their actual power might be limited by innumerable circumstances, but they seemed as titanic as their own creations.

Yet they also seemed to be of common clay, and thus to vindicate triumphantly the Jacksonian claim that any American, given a chance, might prove himself to be the stuff of kings. Although studies show that a significant percentage of business leaders in this period came from successful families, there were enough conspicuously self-made millionaires to sustain the belief that success in America was open to all who were capable. The new nabobs symbolized what the national energies could achieve under liberty and with the help of God and progress. They played their part well, imprinting themselves on the public consciousness by conspicuous expenditure, opulent charities, and open manipulation of allies and rivals in politics and business.

The real history of American business leadership in this era must eventually rest on the study of thousands of unsung managers and owners in a variety of trades and industries. Yet no view of the so-called "Gilded Age" is complete without a brief glance at a few of the tycoons who were interviewed, courted, quoted, sought as patrons, given honorary degrees, immortalized in the christening of ships, streets, schools, buildings, and babies, and not infrequently were elected to legislatures as august as the United States Senate.

Some were gay and gaudy vulgarians, a type especially common among the Pacific Coast miners who struck it rich. Such a man was Colorado's H.A.W. Tabor, who built an opera house for Denver, discovered a portrait of Shakespeare in the lobby, and demanded that it be replaced with his own, crying: "What the hell has Shakespeare done for Denver?" Another ostentatious financier was the corpulent prince of Erie, Jim Fisk, a one-time peddler who bought himself steamboat lines so that he might wear an "admiral's" uniform to work. He also bought an opera house so that he might be, in Vernon L. Parrington's unforgettable phrase, "a patron of the arts—and especially of the artists, if they were of the right sex."

Other tycoons were candidly interested in power rather than the high life, although they lived well enough. Two self-made railroad barons illuminate that pattern. Collis P. Huntington was one of the "Big Four" who "built" the Central Pacific—the western portion of the first transcontinental railroad, completed in 1869. That is, he was one of four Sacramento hardware and grocery merchants—the others were Mark Hopkins, Charles Crocker, and Leland Stanford—who invested in a short line to the gold camps of the Sierras which, eventually, with government loans and subsidies, grew into a line connecting with the Union Pacific in Utah and completing the link across the country. After 1869 the Central's owners used their profits and position to create a new rail system in California, the Southern Pacific, which soon achieved an almost complete monopoly of transport in California, and had ranchers, shippers, courts, and legislatures either battling its influence or dancing to its tune until the end of the century. Huntington outlived the other partners and was, it is generally agreed, the chief planner and decision maker. While Crocker and Hopkins remained engrossed in operational details, and Stanford sought the political footlights (becoming Governor and Senator), Huntington remained backstage and unabashedly fought to control from his office the railroad traffic of the entire Southwest. Like Cornelius Vanderbilt, he enjoyed being a railroad mogul and nothing else. Vanderbilt, whose eighty millions worth of corporate properties included the New York Central in 1877, began life as a ferryboatman from Staten Island. He graduated to ownership of riverboats (whence he derived the title "Commodore") and then railroads. He came to live in a splendid brownstone mansion on New York's Fifth Avenue, and to give his name and a large sum of money to a university in Nashville, but essentially he never changed his roughneck manners or his delight in winning fights by fair means or foul. "Law?" he is alleged to have once said. "What do I care about the law. Hain't I got the power?"

Of quite another stripe was John D. Rockefeller. He was a man of quiet demeanor who had a bookeeper's love for saving fractions of a cent and could apply it to enterprises of imperial grandeur and thus make millions. His Standard Oil Company was the yardstick by which other monopolies were measured in 1890. Rockefeller, actually, was not interested in money for money's sake. He began a career of donations to good causes with weekly gifts of change to the collection plate. At his death he had bestowed hundreds of millions of dollars on higher education, medical research, and religion through institutes and foundations bearing his name. What he liked about a giant business organization was not its power to produce profit but its visible proof of the virtues of order, organization, and planning. When Standard Oil was at its peak, every refiner, every retailer, every engineer, every driller, every railroad president was part of a superb mechanism designed to produce oil and oil products cheaply and copiously. Planless competition, in Rockefeller's view, could not do that. He lived an orderly, comfortable life—almost personifying the rational qualities of his supercorporation as he imposed orderliness on the untidiness of mortality.

One cannot speak of America in the late nineteenth century without mentioning Andrew Carnegie. Born when Andrew Jackson was President, he came to America as a Scottish immigrant, aged thirteen, and first worked in a textile mill. He became successively a telegraph messenger, an operator, a railroad dispatcher and minor official, then a young businessman in the iron and steel trade. At fifty he headed the country's largest steel corporation. In 1901 he sold out his holdings for a quarter of a billion dollars and retired to travel and philanthropy. His talents were literary and persuasive. He got orders for steel by the millions of tons, bought factories, hired experts, stimulated them to incredible feats of production, made his deliveries, and acted as if he were having the time of his life. He wrote books to prove that evolution produced millionaires (ignoring the assistance of the tariff on steel and the inventions of other men in making his own fortune), and to command millionaires to give their winnings to society and die poor. He praised democracy, capitalism, and the Anglo-Saxon people, hobnobbed with friends ranging from Mark Twain to the Emperor of Germany, and was not in evidence when his associates ruined competitors or broke strikes. He did not simply create or use industrial power, he celebrated it and was its advocate.

If Rockefeller was industry's superorganizer and Carnegie was its supersalesman, Junius Pierpont Morgan was its superfinancier. He was not at all self-made. His father was a banker, and he was born to security and securities in 1837. Between 1880 and 1910 he became a specialist in financing industrial reorganizations and combinations through massive loans—and his price always included a share of control of the new corporations, so that he could wage war on wasteful competition (and competitors), which he disliked no less than Rockefeller. In other respects he was quite different from the abstemious Standard Oil magnate, since Morgan frankly lived like a Renaissance prince, spending his money freely on yachts, jewelry, paintings, rare manuscripts, and other aids to good living. Although a devout Episcopalian, he never pretended that the Lord had simply lent him his wealth to be used as modestly and frugally as possible.

All the figures in any gallery of rich men of the 1870s, 1880s, or 1890s radiated a sense of the power inherent in the new forms of production of wealth. Whatever they did or did not do, they seemed to say by their very existence: "Two generations ago, this was a country of a few million souls, most of them farmers. Look on us and see what it has become!" This was their meaning for their contemporaries, who did, indeed, look on them wide-eyed.

THE BENEVOLENTLY NEUTRAL STATE

The victories of big-scale industrial organization were not exclusively the result of machine production and venturesome capitalists. Behind the boom of the postwar years there stood a national government which, at times, actively assisted in the nation's economic modernization and, at other times, was willing to assist business growth by a "hands-off" policy of avoiding taxes and regulations that might hinder the pursuit of maximum profit and thus discourage investment. One long-standing interpretation of the entire Civil War era, in fact, maintains that this linkage between the objectives of businessmen and congressmen was the most significant outcome of the conflict. With Southern planters out of power for a decade and a half—1861 to 1876—Republican leaders, in particular, were able to procure the passage of high protective tariffs, loans and land grants to the railroads, contract-labor legislation allowing the recruitment of low-paid foreign workers, and banking laws weakening the power of agrarian sections to set up their own sources of credit. This was the argument for looking at the war as a "second American Revolution" which confirmed the dominance of "industrial capitalism" over "planter capitalism."

However, like the case for the Civil War as a "cause" of industrial progress, this version of events requires some modification in the light of recent study. The national government in the 1850s had launched exploring expeditions in the polar seas, as well as in the Atlantic and Pacific, whose purpose was not only to gather scientific data but also commercial information. Army surveyors had compiled massive volumes of evidence on the merits of several proposed routes for a transcontinental railroad. An aggressive diplomacy in the Caribbean had shown that the United States was not at all indifferent to the possible future needs of American traders and investors in areas south of the border. The voting on measures to support these operations had not lined up businessmen versus farmers but, instead, had shown many varieties of economic activity, interest groups, and demands. "Agrarian" representatives did not vote as a bloc, but cast their ballots on economic issues according to whether they spoke for large farmers or small, slaveholding or nonslave-holding planters, well-developed sections where industry and agriculture were striking a balance (as in the Ohio Valley) or newer sections still tied to a single-crop economy (as with the states west of the Mississippi). And spokesmen for "business" included bankers, merchants, manufacturers, and transportation executives, who differed widely on the effects of particular governmental acts and policies. The trend toward greater government assistance to economic development was under way well before 1861. Moreover, the wartime Congress of 1862, in which "agriculture" was supposedly a hapless minority, passed the Homestead Act, offering a free 160-acre farm from the public domain to any actual settler. It passed the Morrill Land Grant Act, giving to the states large donations of public land in order to endow agricultural studies in colleges and universities. And it passed the bill creating the Department of Agriculture, although that office did not reach Cabinet rank until 1889. It would seem more accurate to say that the major difference between the Congresses that sat in 1860 and 1862 was that the 1862 Congress had no substantial bloc in its ranks dedicated to fighting for the interests of slavery.

The record shows a pattern of aid to business enterprise which, like certain kinds of embroidery, is boldly visible but not simple in design. The tariff is an example. In 1862 and 1864, Congress passed measures that raised the general level of duties on almost every article imported into the country to approximately 37 percent at first, and then to 47 percent. The 1864 measure was passed with only five days of debate in both houses of Congress. Everyone agreed that the need to raise revenue was critical. What was a wartime emergency policy, however, remained in force uninterruptedly through year after postwar year, but the pressure for retention was drawn from many sources and from both parties. A general ten percent reduction in the level of duties in 1872 concealed the fact that on many individual items the duty exceeded 80 percent of the foreign manufacturer's price—and since domestic prices only needed to match the foreign price plus the duty to be competitive, then as soon as American costs of production dropped to a par with the foreign costs, the duty was almost a gift to the American manufacturer. From 1870 onward, for example, the duty on steel rails was $28 a ton. By 1880, English factories could produce rails at $36 a ton, but the American price was $67, even though American steel was then almost as cheap to make as English. Eventually a number of factors reduced the cost to the consumer of American-made rails but, for a time, the steelmakers had profited very handsomely by their government's barrier to foreign rivals. However, in spite of the demonstrated effect of the duties in raising prices, no massive antitariff protest moved Congress to action before the middle 1880s. Perhaps this was because too many diverse groups shared in the advantages of protection.

Again, it is an oversimplification to say that railroad land grants, like the tariff, were concessions to business need wrung from a reluctant public. The most publicized grant was a donation of twenty "sections" (square miles) of public land per mile of construction, made to the Union Pacific and Central Pacific railroads by acts of 1862 and 1864 to help in the completion of the first transcontinental line. In addition, the lines received loans (not gifts) ranging between sixteen thousand and forty-eight thousand dollars for each mile of finished track. These loans were to be repaid to the government with interest, and the government enforced this provision. In addition, the United States paid only half fare on the subsidized line for moving troops and supplies. This policy of endowing railroad construction was not new, but had commenced by 1850. Long before the Civil War began, nearly twenty million acres of federal land had been dispensed in aid of railroad construction, mainly in the Mississippi Valley. Wartime and postwar grants to three other transcontinental lines, among others, helped to swell the final total of the grants to approximately 130,000,000 acres, but no more grants on this scale were made after 1871. Moreover, they involved less than 7 percent of the national domain in area, although somewhat more in value, and the mileage built with this aid was only one-fifth of the national total as of 1880, when most grants had been finally claimed. The percentages were much higher in the Far Western states most affected by land-grant railroad building, but it should be noted that almost every American in this period believed firmly that the whole nation would be served by bringing western lands, in William H. Seward's words, "into cultivation and settlement in the shortest space of time and under the most favorable auspices." It seemed to make sense to give away a small portion of the nation's landed heritage in order to improve the value of the rest. Only in the hurly-burly of politics twenty years after the Civil War did the cry of "giveaway" to "land monopolists" rise loud in the land.

A similar observation is valid for the Contract Labor Law in 1864, denounced by unions until its repeal twenty-one years later. It did not, as charged, involve the government in the recruitment of cheap industrial labor. The act simply authorized foreign workers to sign contracts binding them to employment in the United States for fixed periods, and made these agreements valid in the courts. The number of these contracts registered with the United States Commissioner of Immigration was small, and while a few skilled workers—particularly in the glass trade—were "imported" by employers, the bulk of the immigrant labor force in factories, railroad work gangs, and mines, was hired from among those who had come to this country without either government or private assistance.

The National Banking Acts of 1863 and 1864 also have been cited as a sign of the government's benevolence toward business. These acts created a system of "national banks," which were to receive charters upon the purchase of certain quantities of United States government bonds. The banks were to deposit these bonds with the Treasury and were to receive, in return, circulating notes. They profited handsomely by lending out these notes at interest and simultaneously collecting interest on the bonds that backed them. More significantly, a prohibitive tax imposed on the notes of state banks reduced the competition of those banks in furnishing currency. Yet one clear purpose of this legislation was to sell bonds for the war, and far from giving favored bankers a monopoly on the issuance of notes, the Treasury put four hundred million dollars of its own paper currency—the famous "greenbacks"—into circulation. Postwar efforts to retire these greenbacks met repeated opposition. A long struggle, lasting until 1896, was opened. Its main issue was whether the government should control and inflate the money supply, and for whose benefit. Its various episodes were triggered by proposed acts for regulating the supply and value of gold, silver, and other forms of money. But the core of the matter is that in this contest battle lines were never neatly drawn between parties, sections, or classes.

In short, it cannot be denied that the tariff, banking, labor, and railroad legislation of the Civil War and Reconstruction years was designed to encourage and assist private enterprise in railroad construction, manufacturing, and the financing of these and kindred undertakings. But such aid was never unlimited, never without some restrictions, and never without support from a broad sampling of the population.

This public approval was entirely natural in view of the country's dominant social outlook. There was almost universal agreement among the men of the 1870s and 1880s that the production of tangible wealth was the chief end of man, that he glorified himself in the acquisition of property, and that the government acted most laudably when it helped him to realize his material ambitions on the widest possible scale. Almost every man in public life was infatuated with the country's material progress, regardless of party or section. In 1884 the Republican Presidential candidate, James G. Blaine, published *Twenty Years of Congress,* a partisan history of national legislation from 1861 to 1881. Blaine concluded with a loving glance at national economic statistics, and declared that rising population and production figures made the era "incomparable," and that "such progress was not only unprecedented but phenomenal. . . It could not have been made except under an industrial system which stimulated enterprise, quickened capital, assured to labor its just reward." The next year there appeared *Three Decades of Federal Legislation* by Samuel Sullivan ("Sunset") Cox, a lifelong Democrat, a work that covered the same span of Congressional history. It, too, concluded with a chest-thumping review of the growth figures in the 1880 census and a declaration that "Our country, with its institutions of benevolence and learning, its wealth, splendor, commerce, and liberties, has become the cynosure of all eyes and the refuge of all lands." Pride in the size of the gross national product went beyond party labels.

Despite these praises, there were numerous Americans who, by the 1880s, expressed strong reservations about the compatibility of the new industrial order with the American theory and practice of liberty and equality. Chapters that follow will show how the economic boom brought about realignment of sectional patterns, producing conflicts that could not be solved by the admission of new states as formerly had been done to balance the interests of slavery and free labor in the Senate. It also was the basis of a shift of power among classes, which could not be reversed by the simple exercise of the ballot. Industrial growth sent men westward and overseas, changed the very shape of their thinking about the society they lived in and its meaning, pitted opposing spokesmen against each other in state and national legislatures and in the courts, and virtually turned the entire history of modern America into the story of a reaction to dynamic economic forces. But in telling that story, we must remember that the men who first saw the light of modern industrialism in America believed that they were included in the dawning of a day not of struggle but of infinite promise.

Chapter III

Urbanization: The Energies of Concentration

To one of the characters in William Dean Howell's novel, *A Hazard of New Fortunes* (published in 1890), the city of New York, as seen from the elevated railway, brimmed with excitement:

> He said it was better than the theatre, of which it reminded him, to see those people through their windows; a family party of work-folk at late tea, some of the men in their shirt-sleeves; a woman sewing by a lamp, a mother laying her child in its cradle; a man with his head fallen on his hands upon a table; a girl and her lover leaning over the window-sill together. What suggestion! what drama! what infinite interest! . . . At Forty-Second Street station . . . the reddish points and blots of gas far and near; the architectural shapes of houses and churches and towers . . . and the coming and going of the trains marking the stations with vivider or fainter plumes of flame-shot steam—formed an incomparable perspective.

But the city was more than a stimulus to artistic vision. In the last half of the nineteenth century, it was the fastest-growing American institution— perhaps the dominating factor in the emergence of today's America. In 1870, only one quarter of the population lived in cities or towns of 8000 or more. In 1960, more than two Americans out of three lived in such places, approximately 125 million out of 180 million people. Moreover, this urban populace was fearsomely concentrated. About 38 million people lived in a single urban belt in the Northeast, running from Boston to Washington, with the suburbs of one major city blending into those of the next.

In 1860, the whole American population was about 30 million. A century later, almost that many people lived in the country's ten largest cities alone. Thirty-eight million more—a number about the size of the entire population of 1870—dwelt in the fast-growing suburbs. The struggle of men to manage their lives through existing social and political institutions in these unbelievable hives is one of the themes of modern life. The rise of the city in late nineteenth-century America was, therefore, a portentous sign of fundamental change.

As patterns of trade and industry shifted, the careers of cities were made and unmade. New York, already rising to the rank of the nation's first city in population, clinched that position in 1898 when its five boroughs were consolidated under one government. Ten years later it had a population of nearly five million. Chicago was a marvel of quick growth. In 1860, it had a population of 109,000; by 1890 it topped one million, and in 1910, with more than two million, it was the country's "second city," a preeminence achieved at the expense of other contenders for the role of the inland capital of the nation such as St. Louis, Milwaukee, and Cincinnati. The great interior basin between the Great Lakes, the Ohio River, and the Mississippi River was a seedbed for urbanization. By 1910, St. Louis, Cleveland, and Detroit were fourth, sixth, and ninth in size (measured by population), while older cities were slipping—Boston falling to fifth, Baltimore to seventh, and New Orleans to fifteenth. Pittsburgh was the major showcase of American heavy industry in the 1890s, but never equaled Cleveland and Detroit in population. Between 1860 and 1910, the Far West produced the cities of Denver and San Francisco out of what had been virtual emptiness. We shall comment later on Southern cities.

But the historian is likely to miss a significant point if he considers only the growth of the largest urban areas. Of greater interest was the increase in the number of small and middle-sized cities in the 10,000 to 250,000 range. These cities increased from 161 in 1870 to 578 in 1910. In the 1880s Omaha grew from 30,500 to 140,000; Kansas City from 60,000 to over 132,000; Wichita from 5000 to 23,000; Duluth from 3300 to 33,100 and Minneapolis from 47,000 to 164,000. The density of the urban population remained highest in the East, but the rate of change from rural to urban living—the growth of the city as a factor in life—was greatest in the old Northwest (Ohio, Indiana, Illinois, Michigan, Wisconsin) and the states bounded by the southern stretches of the Missouri River and the upper reaches of the Mississippi. It was in a region of mills, mines, and factories that an America of inland towns arose, which lured migrants from Europe and from American farmhouses as surely as did New York. Scranton, Wilkes-Barre, Indianapolis, Terre Haute, Springfield, Davenport, Toledo, and hundreds of towns like them, were the theaters of social change. It was

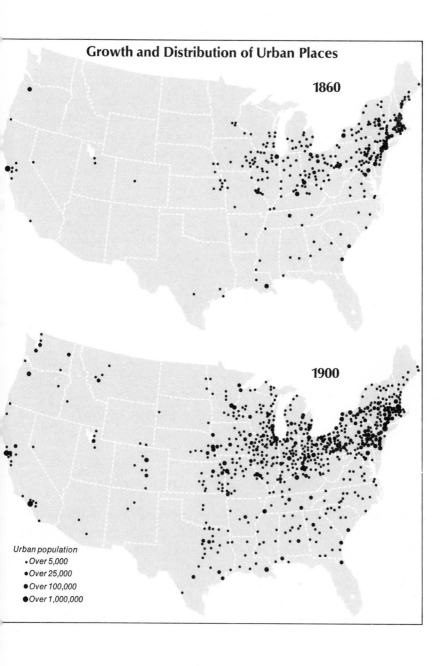

Growth and Distribution of Urban Places

1860

1900

Urban population
· Over 5,000
● Over 25,000
● Over 100,000
● Over 1,000,000

the fusion of this new kind of urban population—four-fifths of it north of the Ohio and Missouri Rivers—into a self-conscious entity that upset political calculations in 1896 and ended forever the old social predominance of agrarianism.

The full story of the urbanization of America must ultimately be written from the yet uncomplete record of life in these middle-sized communities. Standing between the declining countryside and the overshadowing metropolitan giants, these communities experienced a variety of changes that only can be understood after several generations have felt their consequences. The village square became Main Street; the old elite of lawyers, judges, and squires gave way to a new uppercrust of bankers, factory owners and managers, and large-scale retail merchants. The vaudeville theater replaced the revival tent as a scene of entertainment and sociable commingling; the village newspaper yielded to the suburban edition of the nearest big-town sheet; the local schoolmaster was replaced by men (and women) trained in teachers' colleges; the new breed of doctors was also college-trained in faraway places. The companionable grocer stocked more and more prepackaged goods, and the candidates for Congress could no longer shake every hand in the district. The outside world was moving in, at the relentless speed of the locomotives that whisked passengers, mail, and freight in and out of the local depot. The revolution that changed the village into an industrial "Middletown," or a suburb, was beginning. In the twentieth century, the radio, the movie, and the automobile were to accelerate the transformation. Old ways were ceaselessly buffeted by shock waves of change.

INTERNAL COMMUNICATIONS AND POLITICAL POWER

Urban growth pressed unceasingly on traditional ways of organizing a city's political life, and especially on the "internal communications" between the public and its various servants, whose proportion to the rest of the population rose as cities grew larger. Services that were once provided individually or by volunteers—security, fire protection, sanitation, lighting, paving, and a water supply—now required professional departments maintained by the municipal treasury. The construction of necessities such as water-pumping and sewage-disposal plants involved the expenditure of additional millions. Municipal indebtedness grew from 200 million dollars in 1860 to 725 million in 1880, and nearly a billion and a half dollars in 1902. The ratio of expenditure to population grew as the urban community grew.

Inexorably, government became more depersonalized and complex. The citizen, no longer on face-to-face terms with the entire community, could neither debate issues in a town meeting nor elect a few officials to provide for common needs out of modest tax revenues. He cast his ballot for a long list of superintendents and commissioners who, in turn, chose a host of employees and awarded building and other contracts worth millions. The "public" was no longer a small and coherent body aware of how "its" servants functioned, and even the courts, mayors, and councils that were determined to administer the machinery of big-city government honestly could get lost in its intricacies. This was one consequence of urbanism, and one root of the problem of effectively governing the American city, which loomed larger and larger as the twentieth century approached.

Technological improvements, meanwhile, not only changed the face of the city but made possible its very existence on a large scale. It was essential, for example, to move thousands of people daily and rapidly from home to office and factory, and steam and electricity answered this need as even the most willing horseflesh could not. New York pioneered an elevated steam railway in 1870, but in a few years steam yielded to electricity, which posed no fire hazard in crowded streets. The first feasible electrified street rail line opened in Richmond in 1887, and within ten years, 10,000 miles of "trolley" systems were in operation. Although the name belonged, strictly speaking, to a car powered by overhead wires, it was bestowed on cable cars and vehicles drawing their motor current from underground wires as well. Soon there was an entire network of interurban lines, linking cities and creating "streetcar suburbs" that did much to promote real estate speculation, mobility, and the gradual abandonment of the "inner city" as a place of residence. As early as 1873, a Chicago real estate advertisement was declaring that "the controversy . . . as to which offers the greater advantage, the country or the city, finds a happy answer in the suburban idea which says, both . . . the city brought to the country."

The 1880s and 1890s saw still other technological triumphs in meeting the needs of mass populations. Electricity and gas were manufactured and delivered from centrally located stations to homes and shops for power, heating, cooking, and lighting. Steel bridges supplemented steam ferries in spanning rivers. New York's Brooklyn Bridge—a free, lovely creation of

Three of the inventions fostering urban growth—the suspension bridge, the elevated railroad, and the streetcar—converge handsomely in this photograph of the Brooklyn end of the Brooklyn Bridge.

lamp-jeweled roadway, hung by wire cables from stone towers—was a wonder of the age when it was opened in 1887. Steel-framed buildings were developed in the 1880s. Since their outer walls carried no weight and could, therefore, rise high and be freely pierced for windows, these buildings brought a new style to urban architecture. The invention of electric-powered passenger elevators, joined with the strength of the steel framework, made possible the skyscraper and its dramatic upward stretch toward freedom from the crowded street.

Nevertheless, the excitement of urban progress was matched by the gravity of its problems. Where private corporations owned streetcar lines and power plants, they wielded vast influence over a city's life, especially since monopoly was almost the natural form of such huge and costly enterprises. Moreover, traction and utility companies needed official permission in the form of licenses and franchises to construct and operate their systems. Since the potential profit from these franchises was enormous, even conscientious businessmen in the light, power, or transit industries were tempted to secure them by bribing or cajoling municipal officials. Dishonest manipulation of the stocks of these companies was also possible. The fall of man has sometimes been blamed not on Eve or the serpent but on the apple, and the apple in this case was enticing.

"Progress" thus threatened traditional concepts of honest government in the big city by creating an expanded bureaucracy, and putting rich gifts in its keeping. In addition, the electorate was annually swollen by thousands of new voters, many of them newcomers from the countryside or from abroad, knowing little or nothing of municipal problems and machinery. Multitudes of these new urbanites faced acute problems in finding jobs, housing, legal and medical assistance, protection from exploitation by various sharpers, and other indispensable aids to full citizenship. When the civic machinery of a simpler and more self-sufficient day could not help them, poverty, disease, crime, and slum conditions resulted. These conditions were additional consequences of the failure to create, in the big city, a living relationship among citizens, their needs, and their chosen authorities. Into the power vacuum thus formed, there came the institution known as "the machine" and the personage known as "the boss."

THE GOVERNMENT OF LARGE CITIES—BOSSISM AND REFORM

There was one unofficial urban agency that specialized in mobilizing and organizing masses of people. This was the political party. Its workers, bound in a common loyalty to the ticket, were not reluctant to cultivate the humblest new voters. It gathered under one roof hosts of precinct and district workers whose task was to win friends by methods illustrated best in the record of one day in the life of George W. Plunkitt. Plunkitt was a district chieftain of New York's Tammany Hall, a "Social Club" that was actually a Democratic Party headquarters. At 2 A.M. he was roused from bed to bail out a saloonkeeper who was in trouble with the law. At 6 A.M., hearing fire engines, he rushed to the scene, and found clothes and temporary quarters for some of the burned-out tenants.

At 8:30 A.M. he was in the courts, where he paid the fines of several drunks, got some other people discharged by a timely word to the judge, and paid the rent of a family about to be dispossessed. At 11 A.M. he was at home, where he found three men looking for jobs and one who, having been fired, wanted Plunkitt to "fix things up." He spent three hours attending to these matters. At 3 P.M. he attended an Italian funeral, followed by a Jewish confirmation ceremony. At 7 P.M. he presided over a meeting of district captains, reporting on their constituents' current attitudes toward a forthcoming election. At 8 P.M. he showed up at a church fair where he "took chances on everything, bought ice-cream for the young girls and the children, kissed the little ones, flattered their mothers, and took their fathers out for something down at the corner." At 9 P.M. he went to the district "clubhouse," bought tickets for a church excursion and a baseball game, and listened to the complaints of a dozen pushcart peddlers who alleged police persecution. At 10:30 P.M. he attended a Jewish wedding reception and dance.

Plunkitt was no altruist. The result of labors like these was to build up a core of unswervingly loyal voters who would invariably vote for "his" (that is, the Democratic) candidate. Thus able to deliver his district, he was one of the insiders who actually controlled nominations and elections to city offices. These insiders, linked together, constituted a "machine" or "ring" and, where a single man led its members, this man bore the simple but graphic title "the boss."

By crude social services such as Plunkitt's, the machine built its support. But the machine should not be viewed through too much of a haze of sentiment. Since its control of the city lawmaking bodies enabled it to determine appointments, it picked men on the basis of loyalty and donations to its purposes instead of merit on the job. It was able and willing to corrupt judges and election officials, to strong-arm opponents, buy votes, and to pad registration lists with the names of ghosts. (A Philadelphia spoilsman once declared that in his ward, which housed Independence Hall, "the fathers of American liberty voted down here once, and they vote here yet.") It determined who got contracts, franchises, and licenses, arranged the necessary bribes, and it took its own generous and illegal profit from all transactions involving the city. Ultimately, of course, the money came out of the pockets of the taxpayers and consumers. Bossism was not only legally unregulated but was expensive.

Yet the boss often coordinated the efforts of a sprawling officialdom, and businessmen in need of favors were not wholly averse to doing business with him, even though as individual taxpayers and respectable citizens the same businessmen might complain passionately of the graft, shakedowns, and criminality of machine politics. Tammany's boss, Richard Croker, put it succinctly to Lincoln Steffens (then a young police reporter) one day in the 1890s when Steffens asked, "Why must there be a boss, when we've got a mayor and—a council and—" Croker answered:

> "That's why," [Croker] broke in. "It's because there's a mayor *and* a council *and* judges *and*—a hundred other men to deal with. A government is nothing but a business, and you can't do business with a lot of officials, who check and cross one another and who come and go, there this year, out the next. A business man wants to do business with one man, and one who is always there to remember and carry out the—business."

That is an essential fact to bear in mind. In the late 1860s New York's Boss William Tweed and his allies stole millions by authorizing the construction of public buildings at fabulously padded prices and by taking kickbacks from the contractors—but some "honest" firms were undoubtedly involved in supplying the materials. In the same years, Philadelphia was ruled by a so-called "Gas Ring." Its leader, James McManes, moved easily in the respectable society of the city, since he had frequent dealings with companies in which this social group held an interest. Ed Butler's machine in St. Louis in the century's last years also had its blue-ribbon supporters according to Lincoln Steffens.

> Franchises worth millions were granted without one cent of cash to the city, and with provision for only the smallest future payment; several companies which refused to pay blackmail had to leave; citizens were robbed more and more boldly; payrolls were padded with names of nonexistent persons . . . Behind the corruptionists were man of wealth and social standing, who, because of special privileges granted them, felt bound to support and defend the looters.

The machine was, therefore, not simply a tool of larceny. It rightly outraged reformers, yet their assaults on it often failed because they used the wrong approach—either demanding the election of honest officials or the enactment of civil service laws that would take the power of appointment out of political hands. The machine survived these attacks and occasional defeats because its minor officials had struck deep roots in poor communities, and its top leaders performed too many useful services for businessmen. It was the impersonal, costly nature of the big city itself that supported machine politics. After the twentieth century began, municipal reformers who recognized this fact tended increasingly to experiment with new governmental devices such as professional city managers or municipal planning and operating commissions which, in effect, legalized and institutionalized the job of the boss, providing responsibly some of the centralization found under his rule. And, in a sense, the twentieth century state's growing concern with providing essential social services—unemployment insurance, recreational facilities, medical aid for the indigent—is a more systematic formalization of the old-time district leaders' handouts and fixes. The politics of the nineteenth century city played a part in foreshadowing the twentieth century welfare state.

THE CULTURE OF THE CITY

But a city is more than a body politic. It has its own rhythm of existence, its own style of structuring the day and the week. A historian cannot document precisely the human impact of moving from country to city, but he must be aware of the thousands of individual details that underlie the general "facts" of his documents. Farm life had meant rising at dawn, in damp half-light; performing morning chores amid the animal smells of the barn; daytime tasks in the hot fields, punctuated by a heavy mid-day meal; the homeward trudge to supper, settling animals down for the night; and, finally, evening chores—mending tools, utensils, clothes—by kerosene light. In the winter, men and women shared the endless tasks of homemaking indoors. It was a life smelling of soil and vegetation and manure; a life keyed to the animal cycle of sleeping, birthing, waking, and eating. It was an isolated life, and only on occasional Saturdays did going to town bring a change: a buckboard ride, a visit to the hardware and feed and drygoods stores, perhaps a political rally or a revival meeting, a church supper, or other things that brought human contacts outside the family. For solitary recreation there was hunting and fishing—but time for recreation was scarce.

In the city, all was different. The clock ruled. Its alarm rang or the factory whistle blew, and the gaslight flared as people hustled into overalls or "store clothes," ate quickly, and then joined the moving, work-bound mass. There was the ride on horsecar, trolley, or steam ferry over iron bridges and cobbled or paved streets, between walls of brick and stone, grimy factory entrances, tenements (hung with fire escapes and humanity), groceries, laundries, coal and ice stores, clothing stores, and eating houses—all aswarm. The day passed amid the clank of machinery, the murmur of customers' voices, or the buzz of an office. At dusk, the city man went home to dinner, and perhaps the newspaper, and to the sounds of children, quarrels, lovemaking, laughter, and anguish from families who lived ten and twenty to a building and who were separated only by the thinnest walls. Perhaps he took a walk to the corner saloon where knots of men gathered inside and outside, under the streetlamps, and children dodged in and out among feet, pushcarts, horsecarts. In other words, the city offered a life of gregariousness, organization, intimacy, and activity, but it was a life set in motion and stopped by bells and whistles and lights, and a person could be dreadfully alone and anonymous in it.

The bustle, the energy, the architectural magnetism of the city—the forces luring boys from farms like that of the Nebraska family shown on page 79 to the gaslamps—are illustrated in this Chicago scene in front of Carson Pirie Scott & Company.

The city's facilities for structuring nonworking time revealed much about the life style of urbanism. In the city's provisions for leisure, ethnic and class distinctions become sharply visible. To begin with, a large class of poverty-stricken urbanites had virtually no leisure. Persons hard pressed to keep body and soul together could be found in the city in neighborhoods that showed the worst side of urban life. We shall say more about the slums later. In many isolated towns dependent on one industry, the slums consisted of rows of shanties (sometimes company-owned) in tracts without streets, sewers, or lights. In the big cities, especially New York, the word "slum" was synonymous with tenement houses. These were multiple-family dwellings built to squeeze maximum revenue from every square foot of the lots on which they stood. These dwellings, three and four stories high, built around tiny courtyards, and separated by narrow, refuse-choked alleys, failed to provide more than a few lucky tenants with adequate sunlight and air. Moreover, twelve or sixteen families—as many as one hundred and fifty people in that day of large families—shared a single toilet or water-pump, while broken furnaces, lights, and windows were neglected by landlords. City families who were forced by circumstances to live in these quarters— breeding grounds for crime and disease—did not seek leisure but, instead, undertook extra work at home such as laundering, sewing, and cigarmaking, and toiled by lamplight until exhaustion drove them to bed.

For persons a rung higher on the economic ladder, who had a few cents to spare after paying for rent and groceries, the city offered interesting diversions. One diversion, for men only, was the saloon. In 1880, east of the Mississippi, there was one saloon to every 438 persons, in Boston one to every 329, in Cleveland one to every 192, in Chicago one to every 179, in New York one to every 171, and in Cincinnati one to every 124. Although the saloon drew the ire of reformers as being the home of the demon rum, a hangout for "criminal elements," and a natural informal headquarters for the district political machine leader, it nonetheless had positive functions. It was where poor people met for a glass, a game, and some talk. Saloons took on the strongly ethnic flavors of their neighborhoods—Irish, German, or Bohemian. Their back rooms were logical places for lodge, union, and club meetings. A Chicago revivalist even held Sunday school in a saloon after sweeping it out with his own hands. A kind-hearted bartender often gave unemployed and homeless men a night's shelter behind the stove, and a meal from the cheese, pickles, and sausage of the free lunch counter.

Rural virtue also deplored other amusements of the urbanite, such as the billiard parlor, the sweaty little gymnasium where club prizefights were held, and the music halls, vaudeville theaters, and burlesque stages. Popular humor and entertainment in the period from about 1890 to 1917 also filled a need created by city living. The japes and gyrations, the comic skits (at the expense of stereotyped "hayseeds," Irishmen, Jews, "Dutchmen," and Negroes), and the popular ballads contained much that was tasteless and cruel, but they helped to create an identifiable world for the urbanite and to dissolve his own anxieties in laughter. Some of the young mimes and singers who worked on these tiny urban stages—such as Eddie Cantor, Al Jolson, Bert Lahr, W. C. Fields, and Fred Allen—became popular entertainers of the 1920s, when their obvious dissimilarity to respectable, small-town Americans, although sometimes modified by flag-waving and worship of motherhood, appealed to a generation of rebels against Main Street. From the honky-tonks of New Orleans, Memphis, and St. Louis, in the decade before World War I, came ragtime and jazz—jazz being basically a Negro contribution to popular culture. Both were expressions of a refreshing but long unrecognized urban vitality.

The city also offered special advantages to the more ambitious and serious-minded residents. The public library was one example. The Jacksonian reformers who demanded reading rooms and schooling for the children of "mechanics" left an enduring legacy. In 1910 in New York there were 28 branches of the public library in Manhattan, Brooklyn, and Queens, while the main library had 1,722,237 books and pamphlets available to all comers. A program of free evening lectures established in 1888 was flourishing and, during the winter of 1907–1908, 663 lecturers delivered talks in fields such as literature, science, art, and geography to audiences totaling 1,208,336 people. A few other cities did as well. One form of adult education, especially useful to the urban poor, was that provided by the settlement house, a building in the slums usually owned and staffed by volunteer reformers who offered medical and other kinds of assistance to the residents. At Chicago's Hull House (founded by a distinguished humanitarian, Jane Addams, in 1889) or New York's Henry Street Settlement, there were classes in English for immigrants, and also classes for cooking, sewing, nursing, bookkeeping, and other needed skills. In privately endowed night schools, avenues to upward mobility were opened by the schoolbook. One example was New York's Cooper Union, founded by a millionaire businessman and philanthropist, where in the 1870's young immigrant workmen such as Samuel Gompers, a cigarmaker, studied geography, history, commercial law, and economics at night. As head of the American Federation of Labor some years later, he put this knowledge to good use. The settlement-house classroom, the free lecture, and night school were vigorous supplements to the city's formal educational system.

A special agency of popular education, which also flourished in the city, was the daily newspaper. American journalism dates back to the eighteenth century, but the modern "daily" assumed its present form in the 1880s and 1890s. It was then possible to print each day as many as half a million copies of a paper containing many illustrated pages with news less than 24 hours old gathered from around the world and transmitted by cable. Only a century earlier, a colonial printer took a whole day to run off two hundred impressions of a single sheet, folded over to make a four-page paper about the size of a notebook.

Into the mold thus created, editors poured an amalgam of political information, business tidings, notices of social and religious happenings, entertainment, practical advice, and sensation. A generation of aggressive owners and editors, notably Melville Stone of the *Chicago Daily News,* William R. Nelson of the *Kansas City Star,* Charles A. Dana of the *New York Sun,* William Randolph Hearst of the *San Francisco Examiner* and the *New York Journal,* and Joseph Pulitzer of the *St. Louis Post-Dispatch* and *New York World* strove for bigger circulations. Their weapons were comics, political cartoons, reviews, news aimed at women, humorous columns, and good coverage of sports, crime, and scandal. While there were more than 2000 dailies in the nation in 1900, the emulated patterns were set by the most widely read top dozen (located in the biggest cities). These, in their daily quest to interest a mass audience, shaped the view of life of millions, and were a cohesive cultural force unimaginable to an earlier nonurbanized generation.

The wealthy had a life of their own. They lived in elegant homes full of fine furniture and old masters on Chicago's Gold Coast, New York's Fifth Avenue, or San Francisco's Nob Hill and, for recreation, they traveled abroad, drove handsome rigs in the city's parks, or went off to such appropriate watering places as Newport or Long Branch. They kept alive high culture through symphony and opera societies, and the patronage of art galleries, and read magazines geared to middle-class and middle-brow tastes—the *Atlantic Monthly, Harper's, Scribner's, Lippincotts,* and especially the *Century.* These publications told them which were the correct authors and painters, where they should travel, and what the proper reaction was to social problems "created" by immigrants, restless laborers, and machine politicians.

These magazines, addressed to a predominantly female audience, appeared genteel, and yet were silently subversive. Although they drilled the proper young miss in an etiquette as rigid as that of a Chinese court, they also suggested exciting horizons beyond the drawing room. Women were emerging in greater numbers in the labor force at the century's end, with about 3,700,000 working girls in 1890 and nearly 5,000,000 in 1900. The girls who worked in the factories, offices, and schools were driven from home by economic need. Yet their better-off sisters were also tempted to escape from the doll's house, in part, by the prospect of getting out into a world so enticingly described in the popular magazine.

The impact of the city on the church was to call it to battle. When the boss strove for the urbanite's vote, and the editor and advertiser clamored for his attention, the church, perforce, had to struggle for his soul under hard conditions. The mere physical presence of the church amid the urban masses was hard to maintain, as the inner city was abandoned by many congregations whose members moved out to "better" neighborhoods in the face of the incoming lower-class tide. In the areas of maximum population density, the number of houses of worship declined. A horrified student of urban conditions noted that in 1840 Chicago had one church to every 747 inhabitants but, in 1880, it had one to every 2081. In one district with a population of 20,000 under 20 years of age, there were Sunday-school accommodations for less than 2000. The writer was a protestant clergyman who regarded as "unchurched" any area lacking in the protestant ministries that had long formed the backbone of American religious life. He made a vigorous (if not scrupulously logical) connection between this lack and a rising crime rate:

. . . "What wonder that the police arrested last year 7,200 boys and girls for various petty crimes?" The devil cares for them. There are 261 saloons and dago shops [*sic*], three theaters and other vile places, and the Christian church offers Sunday-school accommodation to only 2,000. . . . South of Fourteenth Street, New York, there is a population of 541,000, for whom there is but one Protestant Church to every 5,000 souls.

Overlooking the presence of synagogues and Catholic churches, protestant reformers set out to challenge the devil in the slums. One of their weapons was the "institutional" church—a church that remained in run-down districts and offered not only religious services but programs of recreation and education as well. Another weapon was the rescue mission, which provided clean beds and hot soup to derelicts while workers prayed over them and urged church membership upon them. The American branch of the Salvation Army, founded in 1881, took a major role in this work of redemption, although ever since the 1850s American protestant denominations and the Y.M.C.A. had tried to save young men from what they thought of as the demoralizing temptations of city streets. While the slum preachers sought converts among the "lost" of society, fashionable congregations chose ministers like Henry Ward Beecher, who was up to date, wrote many popular articles, and assured them that divine love ruled the world. This lesson was much easier to impress on successful businessmen than on the tramps and prostitutes in the rescue-mission neighborhoods.

One other protestant institution that was adapted to big-city ways was the revival. In the 1870s Dwight L. Moody, a thick-set, bearded, ex-salesman from Chicago, held a series of wildly successful revival meetings in New York, Boston, Philadelphia, and Brooklyn, and he continued to be the leading American evangelist until his death in 1899. Men and women jammed auditoriums to hear Moody explain that God was only waiting for them to "come home to Him" and be forgiven for their sins. Intermittently Moody's musical associate, Ira Sankey, sang meltingly of lost sheep to the

With word and song Dwight Moody and Ira Sankey exhort a mass audience in 1877 to come to Jesus, in an urbanized version of the old-time camp meeting.

tune of a harmonium. Thousands followed ushers into "inquiry rooms" after the service, accepted Jesus as their savior, and were subsequently enrolled in city congregations. This kind of modification of the old-time camp meeting was part of the urban trend from direct participation in certain functions to vicarious experience. In the canebrakes of Kentucky in 1800, the sinners had testified to their battle with Satan, and jerked wildly in ecstasies like David's before the Ark. Now the audiences listened while the preacher lectured. Moody, devoted and sincere as he was, had made soul-saving a business, complete with planning, advertising, and publicity. In 1887 he even founded a school, the Moody Bible Institute, to train successors.

The devil had his own revivalist in Robert Ingersoll, an enormously popular agnostic lecturer, who filled halls with people who came to hear him talk on subjects such as "Seven Mistakes of Moses." Ingersoll's wide appeal, despite much condemnation from pulpits, lay in the fact that he was, in reality, far from diabolical. He was a devout Republican, a lawyer, who argued cases for corporations, and a believer in home and motherhood and in the perfections of modern science. It may be suggested, in fact, that he preached the one religion that Americans of his day and age really believed.

Thus by 1900 the city presented an exciting kaleidoscope, ranging from its slums and dives to its brownstone palaces, from newspaper offices to political headquarters, from music halls and saloons to busy downtown districts, crisscrossed with overhead wires and cacophonous with the sounds of traffic. The city was undeniably attractive to any youngster of spirit. It was a great crucible that fused immigrants and natives, ruralites and urbanites, classes and masses into an aggregation—fed, housed, entertained, and moved about by miraculous machinery. Its enormous problems, quite unforeseen in the easygoing pre-Civil War era, aroused increasing national concern with each passing year. Yet, despite the alarm it caused, the lusty growth of the city was a brisk stimulus to social invention and a testimony to the vigor and energy of American life after the ordeal of the war.

Chapter IV

Continental and Commercial Expansionism: The Energies of Dispersal (1850–1900)

When Samuel Gompers was a boy in London, he learned a popular ballad that began: "To the West, to the West, the land of the free." The great American West was a magnet to the imagination of those who yearned for a spacious and unsettled landscape, free of civilization's constraints and burdens. But it was more. Exploration showed it to be a rich storehouse of raw materials, awaiting only the touch of invention and capital to be translated into abundant wealth.

These two contradictory themes—the West as the abode of the "natural man," and as the fountain of the abundance that made civilization possible and thus put an end to the "natural man"—teased the American mind almost from the beginning of English settlement in North America. In the nineteenth century, civilization won out. The prizes of a "developed" West were far more tempting and seemed far more promising for the enrichment of American life as a whole than the potentialities of a West that remained innocent, idyllic, and unprofitable.

What prizes they were! The Great Plains, with their seas of grass, were God's own breadbasket for man and animal alike. The various mountain masses, which collectively formed the Rockies, were rich in gold, silver, and copper. So also were the Sierras where the gold strikes first burst into attention. The iron of Minnesota lured trans-Mississippi settlement northward, and the oil and natural gas of the Southwest exerted a parallel pull in the opposite direction. The Pacific slope was thickly covered with timber, laced with river valleys, and seemed to fulfill its ultimate promise in California, parts of which produced wheat, fruit, nuts, wine, and cattle in lavish quantity. There were mountains and deserts guarding these treasures, but they only added to the challenge. In some areas, like the great interior basin of Nevada, Utah, and northern Arizona, nature seemed to block colonization by denying essential water and vegetation. Yet, even there, the Mormons showed that cooperative labor and irrigation could overcome great obstacles.

In the last half of the century, Americans threw themselves upon these riches. In the same period, the technologically and culturally advanced nations of Europe were establishing political and economic domination over the territories of "backward" Asia and Africa in order to tap similar storehouses of raw material, which was indispensable to industry, and to open markets for machine-made products. Americans do not think of themselves as participants in this process of "imperialism" until 1898 but, in fact, well before that date we were staging a similar drama. Our theater of imperial adventure was a contiguous land mass, with provisions made for its division into territories, and final orderly incorporation into the nation as states. Nevertheless, the essential pattern was similar. From the northeast quadrant of the country a stream of machines, dollars, and men flowed into undeveloped areas. Aboriginal populations were uprooted, destroyed, or in effect imprisoned. Resources were exploited on an increasingly massive scale until they threatened to disappear. Much of the profit earned flowed back to the corporate headquarters of the East. A special post-1865 feature of the program was that the South as well as the Far West became a tributary province. Politics in both South and West, therefore, were colored by a new kind of sectionalism. Issues were framed, and leaders were chosen on the basis of their connection with one overriding question: Should there be cooperation with or resistance to the great mining, lumbering, railroad, ranching, merchandising, and banking concerns that called the tune to which the regional economy danced?

When, at the end of the century, the energies of American capitalistic promotion (among other forces) helped to carry American armed men and ships into the Pacific and the Caribbean, it was not a new chapter in our history. It was a continuation of a story begun on our own continent.

THE FUR TRADE AS MODEL, 1820–1850

A glance at the American fur trade before 1850, when it was the trans-Mississippi West's most important economic venture, shows a cycle that was to be often repeated: individual pioneering, then organized effort, followed by expansion, competition, consolidation, depletion and, finally, stabilization. As early as 1809 a group of St. Louis traders had organized the Missouri Fur Company, which sent expeditions following along the trail of Lewis and Clark, to trap beaver. These explorers hoped to establish a base far up the Yellowstone, in a present-day Montana, but had to settle for operations restricted to the lower stretches of the Missouri. John Jacob Astor's American Fur Company, in 1810 and 1811, sent parties by land and sea to establish a post on the Columbia River in Oregon, immodestly named Astoria. The British captured it, however, in 1812, after which Astor sold it to the powerful Canadian North West Company.

But the fate of Astoria did not dampen American interest in Far Western furs. In 1824 William Henry Ashley, a Missouri politician, speculator, and expansionist, organized a company of trappers and traders to penetrate the Central Rockies. He sent out a preliminary party under Jedidiah Smith, who discovered South Pass and sent back a train of packhorses loaded with pelts. The next year Ashley himself went as far as Utah's Green River, and devised a basic method of operation that avoided the need for building and maintaining forts at the limit of westward advance. This was to send out parties of trappers who lived off the country all spring, while hunting the beaver, and then gathered at a rendezvous point for a riotous period of selling furs and securing fresh trade goods brought out by caravan from the settlements. The goods included knives, guns, hardware, blankets, clothing, tobacco, and abundant whiskey. After a protracted debauch, the trappers would head back toward the mountains to make winter camps and await the spring thaws of the next year.

These mountain men, only a few hundred in number, were incredibly tough and skilled. A Jim Bridger, Thomas Fitzpatrick, Jim Clyman, Joseph Walker, or Kit Carson was more than a fur hunter and trader. He was the master of a demanding craft. As Bernard DeVoto points out:

> He had to live in the wilderness . . . To read the weather, the streams, the woods; to know the ways of animals and birds; to find food and shelter; to find the Indians when they were his customers or to battle them from stump to stump when they were on the warpath and to know which caprice was on them; to take comfort in flood or blizzard; to move safely through the wilderness, to make the wilderness his bed, his table, and his tool—this was his vocation.

He was also the geographer of the vast solitudes that were the interior of North America, and he learned to thread them long before engineers and mapmakers gave them fixed and familiar names and forms for travelers. In 1823 Jedidiah Smith discovered South Pass. In 1825 another trader, Peter Skene Ogden, found Great Salt Lake, and the following year Smith blazed a trail from there to California. Joseph R. Walker opened another trail to central California in 1833, making the first east-to-west crossing of the Sierras in the process. To the southward, Sylvester Pattie in 1827 found the way from Santa Fe to San Diego by way of the Rio Grande, the Gila, and the Colorado. Along Idaho's Snake River or Nevada's Humboldt, and wherever settlers were later to trace the route westward to California or Oregon in the security of a known route, the mountain men had left their footprints.

But they were also participants in a business, and the inexorable rules of business shaped their careers. Ashley's interests were eventually sold out to a larger concern, the Rocky Mountain Fur Company. This company, in turn, like others of its kind, was challenged in 1831 by the American Fur Company whose great resources were too much for the rival mountain men. By 1834 it had driven these victors over the wilderness from the economic battlefield. Then, in an inexorable process that saw large firms yield to larger firms, the Hudson's Bay Company, which had absorbed its Canadian competitors, also moved in. By 1840, even the American Fur Company retreated before it, and sent no more caravans into the mountains. The rendezvous system was abandoned. In any case, the streams were trapped out. The small amount of trading that continued was done at permanent, settled posts. By 1846, the once-empty fastnesses were alive with the white-topped wagons of migrants on the way to become farmers in Oregon or California. Adventure, at last, yielded completely to business.

Thus an economic attraction had led brave men into a hostile territory, which they "developed" by opening it to further settlement. As profits were returned, individual capitalists were tempted into speculative ventures. They were followed by large and powerful organizations well-financed from non-Western sources, who eventually dominated the scene. Finally, the bonanza had come to an end, and what remained was the unromantic production of a commodity. This was the pattern to be repeated again in the mining and cattle-raising industries, where prospector and puncher would flourish as the trapper had flourished and, in turn, would yield to the promoter. In the long run, it was capital that tamed the wilderness and reaped its rewards.

RAILS AND MINES, 1850–1885

The ultimate development of the Far West, however, was not really possible until the technical marvel of the age—the railroad—reduced the awesome Western distances to manageable journeys for men and freight. Between 1850 and 1873, lines were built that spanned the distance between the Mississippi and Missouri rivers, connecting St. Louis and Kansas City, Chicago and Council Bluffs, and other important cities in Missouri, Iowa, and Kansas. Other lines linked Chicago with Minneapolis and St. Paul. All were substantially aided by state and local land grants and loans.

But the grand design was to span the continent, and it inflamed imaginations from the earliest days of railroading. In 1845 Asa Whitney, a New York merchant, petitioned Congress to support construction of a railroad from Lake Superior to the valley of the Columbia. Although such a line would run through almost entirely unoccupied country, Whitney was a commercial imperialist, who viewed the venture as iron link in a chain of richly profitable trade between New York and the Orient. Congress declined to implement Whitney's vision of teas, silks, and spices whirling across North America but, during the 1850s, it continually debated the question of what backing the country should give to a transcontinental line or lines. All specific projects, however, fell afoul of sectional antagonisms. It was impossible to agree on a northern, southern, or central route for the road. In 1862, however, land grants and loans were authorized for a line to be built by two companies—the Union Pacific, building westward from Omaha (just opposite Council Bluffs on the Missouri), and the Central Pacific, coming eastward from Sacramento.

A seven-year epic of construction followed—a triumph of the nineteenth century's technological imagination fertilized by government financing. Armies of engineers, surveyors, mule skinners, and section hands (including thousands of Chinese recruited by the Central Pacific) chipped, blasted, and drilled tunnels through mountains that were supposedly impassable, and laid mile after mile of track across deserts and prairies known previously only to the buffalo and the redskin. Every rail, spare part, pound of blasting powder, side of beef, and packet of tea had to be brought by water and land to the railheads. The cost and scale of the undertaking were stupendous. When the lines finally joined in 1869 at Promontory Point, in Utah, the nation justly celebrated: "Chicago made a procession seven miles long; New

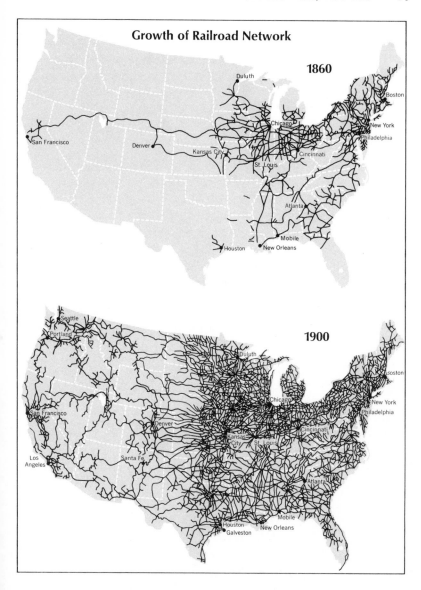

Growth of Railroad Network

1860

1900

York hung out bunting, fired a hundred guns, and held thanksgiving services in Trinity; Philadelphia rang the old Liberty Bell."

But the completed Union Pacific was only the first line to span the country.

In 1883 the Santa Fe completed connections by purchasing old lines and building new ones, between St. Louis and Needles, on the California-Arizona border. From this point it joined the tracks of the Southern Pacific and gained access to San Francisco and Los Angeles. A third route was completed when the Southern Pacific built eastward to El Paso, Texas, to join other lines with connections to New Orleans. Almost simultaneously, the Northern Pacific, linking St. Paul and Duluth with Portland, Oregon, was finished. By 1885 there were four transcontinental lines. A fifth was added in 1893 with the opening of the Great Northern which, more or less, paralleled the Northern Pacific.

Between these various trunk lines, a network of feeder roads gradually spread until the "inaccessible" west was no longer a land of isolation. Cities such as Boise, Denver, Tucson, Laramie, Butte, and Albuquerque were now but a two or three days' trip from the settled regions of the country. The actual impact of the roads on the patterns of Western settlement and economic activity varied. They were probably more important, for example, in encouraging farmers to settle on the Great Plains than in populating the mountain states. But their psychological effect was probably profound. They destroyed the idea of the West as remote and untouched by civilization, and thus fostered both further settlement and the belief that an era of unlimited freedom to pioneer was closed.

Certainly the locomotive's conquest of the West signified the doom of the unfettered red man with the Great Plains as his hunting ground. As the rails advanced, the Indians receded. Between 1863 and 1887, major Indian campaigns were fought against the Navajo, Apache, Cheyenne, Arapaho, Kiowa, Comanche, Nez Perce, and Sioux tribes, inevitably ending in the Indians' defeat and in their restriction to smaller reservations. In 1887 the government put a capstone on the process by passage of the Dawes Severalty Act. This empowered the President to divide the lands of any tribe and give 160 acres to Indian heads of families, who were to secure final title to the land and be made citizens of the United States after a twenty-five year probation period. While, in one respect, it represented an attempt to civilize the Indian and bring him into the white man's way of farming, in another it aimed a blow at the communal organization that underlay Indian life. In attempting to destroy tribal unity, the act, although hailed by some reformers as humanitarian, succeeded in enforcing dependence upon the red men who had once been huntsmen, wanderers, and lords of the land that sustained them. (The principle behind the act would be abandoned in the twentieth century.) While the Indian wars were in progress, a wholesale slaughter of the buffalo herds, on which the Plains Indians depended for life itself, virtually wiped the animal from the face of the earth. (In 1903, only 34 herds were known to be in existence.) It was symbolic that as the locomotive became king, the Indian brave became a tamed receiver of handouts, and the buffalo disappeared. Nature was no match for power.

Meanwhile, the opening of the West was accelerated by the same interest in precious metals that had led men to the New World itself. The California gold discoveries of 1849 were portentous enough. They not only turned a newly won territory into a state within two years, but they also boosted national gold production from 484,000 fine troy ounces in 1848 to 3,144,000 in 1853. Thereafter, California annually produced between two and three million ounces (except for two years) until 1871. Gold rushes also took place in Colorado and Nevada in 1859, in Arizona in 1862, in Idaho and Montana between 1862 and 1866, and in South Dakota's Black Hills as late as 1874. Even more significant for future political and economic history were the tremendous yields of silver that also were found along with the gold. Silver production in 1859 was a mere 77,000 fine troy ounces. In 1861 it topped a million and a half, by 1862 it was up to 3,480,000 (at an average New York price of $1.35 an ounce), at the Civil War's end in 1865 the annual output was 8,701,000, and ten years later it was 24,530,000 at $1.24 an ounce—better than thirty million dollars' worth in a single year. In 1893 production had climbed to a dizzying 60,000,000 ounces but, by then, the price had sagged to approximately seventy-eight cents. Out of these figures was born a curious voting alliance of the 1890's, favoring the unlimited coinage of silver, between debt-ridden and inflation-minded farmers and multimillionaire mine owners in quest of a government-supported market.

In mining, as in the fur trade, there was a relentless transition from individual to corporate initiative. In the early gold rush days, a lone prospector could work streams with the most primitive tools—a pan in which to slosh the mud of a river bed back and forth spilling the lighter dirt and silt over the edge, and leaving the heavier nuggets of gold in the bottom; or a "cradle," which increased the quantity of earth that could be "washed" in this way. Several miners might build a crude sluice—a wooden trough through which a running stream was diverted to wash still larger loads of soil, while the gold was trapped by wooden cleats. With these uncomplex tools, the field was open for anyone to try his luck, and by the thousands they did. Not everyone became a millionaire, but a day's work could produce fifty or sixty dollars' worth of gold. The miner took this gold into town where shrewder men struck real pay dirt by selling him blankets, tools, dinners, and drinks at fantastic prices; for example, chickens at $5 apiece, flour at $28 a hundredweight, and butter at $1.20 a pound.

But this was in a primitive stage. After surface deposits were exhausted, gold and silver had to be dug out of the bowels of the mountains. This process involved cutting and hauling thousands of feet of timber to shore up galleries, providing fans for ventilation, pumps for drainage, and transporting the ore over long distances to refineries. Refining itself was a machine process, requiring that the ores be crushed, dissolved in chemicals, and then evaporated to recover the dissolved gold and silver. This required money in large quantities. Therefore, after 1860 in Nevada, prospectors who were "smitten with the silver-fever," in the phrase of Mark Twain (who was there at the time, and whose *Roughing It* is a classic description of the time and place), did not themselves plan to mine but hoped to discover and then sell valuable claims. The saloons of Virginia City or Gold Hill resounded with the voices of men trading in "feet"—portions of a claim to a vein of ore—in gaudily named mines like the Ophir, the Grand Mogul, the Bunker

Gold mining, by 1859, was already becoming a gang operation, as shown by these several buildings and the group of miners, dwarfed by the terrain, in a California digging.

Hill or, more prosaically, the Gould and Curry. There was something magnificent about these men in clay-stained work pants, sleeping in tents and crackerbox shanties, airily expecting to be millionaires by morning. Few succeeded, but the prospect was always there, since a profitable mine was a cornucopia: the Consolidated Virginia produced two hundred million dollars' worth of silver for various owners; the Bunker Hill and Sullivan (in Idaho) produced two hundred and fifty million dollars' worth.

The fact remained that mining had become an aspect of industry. By the 1880s dozens of companies owned producing mines, and an increasingly large share of the profit of the business came from financing the transportation, refining, and marketing of the mines' output. The prospectors who were both lucky and astute invested their winnings in banks, express companies, or land, while increasingly the actual mining was conducted by gangs of dollar-a-day laborers. The mining monarch of the century's end never handled a pick or pan. He was Meyer Guggenheim, a Philadelphia businessman, who invested in two bankrupt Colorado mines (the "A.Y." and the "Minnie"). He got them into production again, moved into the refining end of operations, and by 1910 had created (with his sons) a world-wide corporation whose agents probed the earth for gold, silver, coal, nitrates, and diamonds in South America, Africa, and Alaska. Likewise in the 1880s the best copper-mining properties, representing enormous wealth, eventually fell into the hands of three powerful businessmen—Marcus Daly, Frederick A. Heinze, and William A. Clark—who, in turn, were replaced as chief powers in the state by Anaconda Copper, a combine created after 1900. The engineer, the banker, and the chairman of the board became the men who directed the exploitation of mineral resources on a modern scale. Mining kings like Clark or California's George Hearst were elevated to the Senate amid loud charges of vote-buying. Strikes became a bloody feature of mining-town life. These developments, too, were part of the meaning of industrial penetration of the virgin West.

THE CATTLE KINGDOM

While enterprise tunneled the mountains for gold and silver, the forces of expansion were also feeding on the magnificent endowment of free grazing land constituting the Southern Great Plains. A simple equation furnished the initiating energy. Texas was full of cattle in 1865—descendants of mingled

These two photographs represent the two faces of the cowboy. The bronco-buster of the statue by Frederick Remington is all dynamic action befitting the romantic legend. The sleepy cowhands preparing to go on night-guard depict the prosaic activities of hired hands in the cattle industry.

American and Mexican herds. Tough and wiry, the longhorns fattened in unfenced freedom on the abundant prairie grasses. In Texas they were worth four or five dollars a head. The meat-hungry cities of the upper Mississippi Valley, however, were ready to pay as much as forty dollars for a steer. To bring the four-dollar animal to the forty-dollar market was an opportunity and a challenge. The railroads sharpened the challenge by extending westward

from St. Louis, Kansas City, Chicago, and other packing centers to points in western Missouri and central Kansas: Sedalia on the Missouri Pacific; Abilene on the Kansas Pacific; and Dodge City on the Santa Fe.

The way to wealth was to gather a herd and drive it overland from range to railhead and, for this task, a special worker—the cowboy—came into existence and soon became legendary. Half a dozen "punchers" could herd a thousand steers over hundreds of miles of open territory, braving heat, dust, storms, stampedes and other hazards. These included Indians, inclined to help themselves to free beef, and sometimes Kansas and Missouri farmers who objected when the trail crossed their lands and who argued their property rights with shotguns. The endurance and horsemanship of the cowhand were remarkable, and his workaday costume was transmuted by imagination into the very stuff of romance. The broad-brimmed hat (a sunshade), the neckerchief (a dust mask), the chaps (to protect pants from snagging on brush), and the high-heeled boots (for better management of the stirrups) transformed an agricultural employee working on the herd owner's behalf for $30 a month, plus bacon and beans, into the last knight to ride free in the virgin emptiness of the West. Unfettered by law or social custom, he nevertheless was supposed to live by a self-policed code of loyalty and purity that made him the archetypal "good guy," free of lust, greed, and self-doubt, and even able to kill with a pure heart because he killed only when confronted unavoidably with unalloyed evil. For documentation, we may read a thousand novels (the prototype is Owen Wister's 1902 *The Virginian*) or see as many Western movies or television programs. The actual cowboy was doubtless more prosaic than the image (although he liked to dress the part for visitors), and his trail-end sprees in the cow towns were remote from Sunday-school morality. But he was, like the mountain man, one of the last individualists in a society whose texture was rapidly hardening. Ironically, like the other pioneers, he was helping to close in the wide open spaces.

For inevitably, the success of the first overland drives in the late 1860s bred emulation. Over the Chisholm, Sedalia, and Western trails, armies of horned beasts marched each spring; between 1868 and 1871 the Abilene yards alone loaded nearly 1,500,000 Texas beefs. Gradually the range cattleman's area of operations moved northward and westward, into Kansas, Nebraska, Colorado, Wyoming, Montana, and the Dakotas. Cheyenne and Bismarck became the towns where cattle were loaded aboard trains to be shipped back eastward for butchering (sometimes with a pause to be fattened up on Iowa corn after the rigors of the trail). The five states and territories mentioned had a total cattle population of approximately 130,000 in 1860 and more than four and one half *million* twenty years later. Inevitably the range began to be overgrazed, and associations of cattlemen fought each other over water rights and brands. The more farsighted among them sensed the end of the open range and began to acquire title to ranch lands. This, of course, required capital, as did the initial purchase of starter herds, and corporate funds began to enter the picture—some of them European in origin. In Wyoming alone in 1883, twenty stock-raising corporations, capitalized at twelve million dollars, were formed. In England and Scotland companies like the Prairie Cattle Company invested in herds and ranches, and American meat prices became a subject of interest in financial circles in London.

Inevitably there was a downfall. In the middle 1880s prices began to tumble and, in the winters of 1885–1886 and 1886–1887, fierce blizzards ravaged the northern herds. Other forces closed in on the freewheeling open-range cattleman. The advance of the railroads eliminated the need for the long drive, and also brought out thousands of farmers whose fences cut across the trails. The free grass was fast disappearing, and the optimistic adventurer, who had bought herds on credit when steers brought fifty dollars each, found himself in bankruptcy court when they fetched only ten dollars. As these marginal operators were squeezed out, success went to the well-financed companies and individuals who fenced the land they bought, grew and stockpiled supplies of winter feed, and wisely bred animals that yielded more choice cuts and less sinew. The businessman-rancher replaced the old hell-for-leather cowman (but did not discard his vocabulary or garments), and the cowboy spent more time mending fences and cutting hay than he did in the saddle. The bonanza of free grass—like the gifts of abundant beaver and rich veins of ore—brought out the individual adventurer but, in the end, it was the organizer who was in command when the first showers of easy wealth dried up. The cattle kingdom's rise proved, once again, that the ultimate profit from the resources of the West went not to those who first tapped them but to those who undertook their production in quantity, their processing into finished goods, their transportation, and their sale. This was a lesson that began to grow on Great Plains settlers in the 1890s, and by the time the West was carved into states—Colorado was admitted in 1876, Washington, Wyoming, and the Dakotas in 1889, and Idaho and Montana in 1890—the lesson was having some political effects. The early twentieth-century careers of Western battlers against the railroads and the trusts, such as California's Hiram Johnson, Idaho's William E. Borah, Nebraska's George Norris, and Montana's Burton K. Wheeler, were shaped by the youthful response of these men to economic developments in the West between 1875 and 1900.

THE NEW SOUTH

The post-Reconstruction South deserves scrutiny in this connection since, even though it had its separate and special problems, it too became to some degree a dependent section, developed by the expansive energies of north-eastern capitalism and paying a high price for the development. The South's transition to this status was presided over by the state governments, which inherited power at the end of Reconstruction. Their leaders were a new breed. Unlike the prewar planters who had looked on the tariff and federally financed internal improvements as twin horses drawing the cart of Union to destruction, the spokesmen for the restored South welcomed the bank and the factory to the section. They were believers in the philosophy of progress through economic development under government protection and encouragement, especially to investors. They were often directors and shareholders in railroad, mining, lumbering, and manufacturing companies. A representative statesman of the new South was Georgia's Joseph E. Brown, who served as both Senator and Governor in the 1880s and, in addition, was president of the Western and Atlantic Railroad, the Southern Railway and Steamship Company, and the Walker Coal and Iron Company. These men sang the old litany concerning the benevolent effects of industrial diversification in breaking the South's dangerous dependence on cotton for prosperity. The trouble was that the theory worked only when new enterprises returned revenue to the section—profits for local investors, wages for workers, and taxes for the states. But Southern states after the war often invited industries to locate by means of generous tax exemptions, undercut any hope of decent wage levels by leasing convicts as laborers for pennies a day, and took no steps to control the lobbying and manipulation of out-of-state corporations which owned the South's industries and got most of the returns.

The railroads were evidence of how an economic blessing within the section could primarily enrich outsiders. Lines ramified rapidly in the 1870s and 1880s; the section's total mileage jumped from approximately 16,000 miles in 1880 to more than 40,000 in 1890. The roads were supposed to break the South's isolation, link her to national and world markets, and pump health into her economy. But promise outran reality. Many of the lines had been built during Reconstruction with the assistance of lavish gifts of state bonds. When the payment dates on these came due, state treasuries were hard-pressed to meet their obligations. In several states, battles broke out between advocates of paying the bonds off at full value and persons who wanted to repudiate or scale down the debts. (This was a striking revival of the old argument between Hamilton and his opponents in George Washington's first administration.) The "readjusters," who wished to pay less than face value, buttressed their arguments with liberal evidence of fraud in the issuing of the bonds and profits made in connection with the roads which more than compensated the bondholders. The partisans of "state credit" warned that venture capital would be frightened away forever by anything less than full payment. In Virginia, a Readjuster party won control of the state government in 1879; elsewhere the results of the battle were inconclusive. Wherever it appeared, however, the railroad bond question sharpened class antagonisms within the South, echoed the "honest money" issue agitating the whole country, and indicated that the Southern people were paying dearly for the advantages of steam transportation. Nor was the situation improved much when the inevitable dynamics of consolidation affected Southern railroads. By 1886 one corporation, the Richmond and West Point Terminal Company, controlled about 8500 miles of Southern line and, of its twenty directors elected in 1890, seventeen lived in New York. The depression of 1893 led to further bankruptcies which, in turn, led to a reorganization financed by J.P. Morgan, who ultimately dominated three major consolidations—the Southern Railway, Atlantic Coast Line and Seaboard Air Line—which encompassed the fattest part of the Southern rail net. Morgan was no Southerner.

Likewise, the penetration of northern Alabama, with its coal and iron deposits, by the railroads spurred interest in a Southern iron and steel industry. By 1890, Birmingham was on its way to becoming "the Pittsburgh of the South." Eventually, however, the independent companies that had pioneered in the development of the region were swallowed up in combinations, the biggest of them being the Tennessee Coal and Iron Company, which was bought by the Morgan-controlled United States Steel Corporation in 1907. The directors of United States Steel, however, were not inclined to let their Southern mills undersell their Northern firms in the profitable line of finished steel products. They set prices of Southern steel products on a differential basis—the cost at Pittsburgh, plus transportation charges from Pittsburgh to the consumer (even when he bought the shipment from Birmingham), or cost plus a flat rate that gave Pittsburgh a competitive edge. Alabama's place in the system was to ship raw iron northward for finishing. Southern lumber and textiles were also sent out of the section for final processing. The industries of the restored section were, as the region's best historian notes, "of one general type—the 'low wage, low-value-creating industries.'" Southern spokesmen were not backward in pointing out the advantage of the low-wage characteristic to northern businessmen. During a great railway strike that tied up northern cities in 1877, a North Carolina journal spoke of the "peaceful, self-contained attitude of the Southern states" in contrast with the "convulsed and panic-stricken, mob-ridden states of the North." What that meant in terms of dollars and cents was revealed by census figures, which showed that in 1909, for example, the average wage of a Southern worker was 12 percent less than elsewhere in the country—$452 per year against $518. And Southern resources as well as Southern labor were proffered freely; gigantic land grants were made to Northern and foreign investment companies for mining and lumbering purposes, and when there were murmurs against a rapid exhaustion of these resources, the typical retort was that of a Tennessean: "Such stuff, if taken seriously would leave all nature undisturbed. As for these investments of Northern capital, the South is glad to have it come. . . . We welcome the skilled lumberman with the noisy mill."

A great propagandist of the New South, Henry W. Grady, editor of the *Atlanta Constitution,* had drawn glowing word pictures in the mid-1880s of a South busy with the manufacture of iron, lumber, clothing, tobacco, furniture, and cottonseed oil—a contented land of industrious workers and prosperous farmers. But outside of the South's few cities, the dream failed to harden into fact. In 1900 the estimated per capita wealth of the United States was $1165; of the South, $509 or less than half. The state governments that invited industries to come Southward tax-free simultaneously cut expenditures for schooling, prisons, asylums, roads, bridges, and hospitals to the bone. Grady's factories were there. Production statistics climbed steadily between 1880 and 1910, and expositions were held in places such as Dallas, New Orleans, and Atlanta to celebrate the achievement. But the "New South" remained generally impoverished.

Feeling the impoverishment at its worst was the Southern farmer, still bound to cotton and desperately in debt to the merchants who provided seed, tools, work animals and their furnishings, fertilizer, and meal on credit at tidy markups. Tenantry was common. On the surface, the prewar plantations appeared to have been broken up, but many holdings that appeared as "farms" in the census returns were actually not owned by their cultivators. They were leased in return for a share of the crop. And the cropper's own share was often pledged to the merchant as security for loans. The so-called "crop lien" system of credit kept Southern agriculture tied to cotton even when overproduction and toppling prices were clearly the result. (It was less than five cents a pound in 1894.) Small wonder that by 1910 in eight Southern states, tenants constituted more than half the farm population. The dream of a free yeomanry—in whose name the great crusade against the Slave Power had been conducted—was dead in most of the South.

The squalor in which many white farmers existed was even worse and more widespread among the Negroes, whose problems we shall examine in the next chapter. Yet to challenge the system of exploitation at the polls was impossible for the Negro and was difficult even for the rural white.

This sharecropper's shack in Arkansas photographed in the 1930's, is little better than the slave huts at the Hermitage Plantation in Georgia (top). The similarity illustrates the severe and long-lasting economic retardation of the South after 1865.

He had to fight for better roads and schools, agricultural extension services, a lifting of tax burdens, liberalized credit, control of railroad rates, and fairer prices for his goods within the confines of the Democratic party. This was a limitation enforced by a confining post-Reconstruction orthodoxy which insisted that any challenge to existing leadership was an affront to the Confederate dead, and would, by dividing the Democratic party, break white solidarity and restore the "horrors" of "Negro rule." The resulting one-party dominance deprived dissenters of much hope. Ill-housed, ill-fed, and ill-clad, the Southern poor white paid heavily for his "supremacy." Nevertheless, he did begin to make tentative thrusts at power in the 1880s and 1890s, which became part of the story of Southern Populism.

The South, on the whole, remained insulated from many of the changes transforming the nation. It was proud of its low rate of urbanization and immigration, and its resulting homogeneity and conservatism. It had its showcase cities like New Orleans, Atlanta, Memphis, Louisville, and Nashville, and a handful of state universities. Basically, however, it remained "the Bible belt," largely sealed off from sophistication, high standards of public health and learning, and from the variety and ferment of the national culture. Underlying this was the white South's own collective official worship of a nonexistent "happy time" before the Civil War, and its false attribution of all its problems to Reconstruction. These attitudes evaded the grim fact that it was an economic province in bondage, well described by C. Vann Woodward:

> . . . . The immemorial pattern of colonialism—the dependence upon the sale of cheap raw materials on a world market and upon buying back manufactured goods from protected industries and commercial areas—continued to hold sway in the South despite the much-vaunted "industrial revolution." Everywhere it was the pattern for poverty.

PALM AND PINE: THE EARLY PHASE

The same energies and ambitions that set men to building railroads in California or Alabama, digging for silver in Nevada or coal in Alabama, building refineries in Colorado and cotton mills in the Carolinas, and financing the purchase of grazing lands in Wyoming or stands of timber in Florida were at work elsewhere. Commercial adventurers dreamed of teaching Asia's teeming millions to eat wheat bread and canned corned beef by kerosene lamplight and to wear Yankee-made cotton shirts and leather boots. Other speculators counted potential revenues of mines and railroads in Mexico. Still others saw harvests of dollars in the sugar and pineapple plantations of Cuba and Hawaii. These visions were the fuel of expansion in many directions—not only westward, but southward and abroad.

The national government encouraged hopes like these after the war. In 1861 the State Department became the office of William H. Seward, the eloquent apostle of the "higher law" which predicted that slavery would inevitably fall before the advance of the railroad, the telegraph, the common school, the factory, and the free press. Having seen this prediction borne out, Seward attempted to extend the area of American influence and trade into the Pacific by the purchase of Alaska and annexation of Midway Island in 1867. Seward's vision was good. Neither territory had any apparent value at the time of purchase (Alaska's mineral wealth was still unexplored), but both territories offered bases and harbors for American merchant and naval vessels in the North and South Pacific, respectively.

In 1869 and 1870, President Grant requested Congress to annex San Domingo, whose government, under the influence of American investors and promoters, had requested the step. The President frankly asserted that "San Domingo will become a larger consumer of products of Northern farms and manufactures." Antiexpansionist sentiment, however, defeated the plan. But commercial penetration of the Pacific, with diplomatic assistance, continued, unaffected by the change in administrations from Republican to Democratic in 1885, back to Republican in 1889, and back again to Democratic in 1893. A treaty of reciprocity was signed with Hawaii in 1875; a naval coaling station in Samoa was leased in 1878, and the islands later (in 1899) became a protectorate of the United States, Great Britain, and Germany; and a commercial agreement with Korea was signed in 1882. In 1893, American settlers in Hawaii, chiefly descended from planters and missionaries, overthrew the weak native government, set up a republic, and clearly hoped that commercial advantage and sentiment would lead the United States to annex them as it had done earlier with Texas. This finally occurred in 1898. In Latin America, the steady rise of American investments in sugar, cocoa, and fruit plantations, as well as in mines and railroads, aroused the attention of James G. Blaine, Secretary of State in both the Garfield (1881) and Harrison (1889–1893) administrations. Blaine not only intended to protect these investments but vigorously promoted reciprocity treaties to increase Pan-American trade, certain that this would "stimulate the demand for articles which American manufacturers can furnish with profit." This idea was stated succinctly, with regard to Asia, by the American minister to China, Charles Denby, who remarked in a letter in 1885: "Fancy what would happen to the cotton trade, if every Chinese wore a shirt." The severe depression in 1893 led some economists to wonder whether the cause lay in an American industrial machine already turning out a surplus that could not be consumed, in which case overseas markets would then be the necessary safety-valve for the economy. (It was in troubled 1893, too, that a historian, Frederick Jackson Turner, said in effect that the free land of the frontier, rapidly disappearing, had been such a safety valve for American society, as a whole, up until 1890.)

The consequences of commercial expansion were far-reaching. Advocates of increased naval power to protect our trade succeeded in persuading Congress to begin to modernize the American fleet, which had lapsed into obsolescence following the Civil War. The prospect of close contacts with the dark-skinned races of the world pricked the imagination of certain believers in the doctrines of "social Darwinism." Writers such as Josiah Strong, a Congregational clergyman and social critic, speculated as to whether the Anglo-Saxon race, gifted with the powers of invention and self-government, and the correct interpretation of Christianity, might not have a divine mission to bring the light to the rest of the globe. In 1891 Alfred Thayer Mahan, a naval officer lecturing at the Naval War College, published *The Influence of Sea Power on History,* in which he proved that the greatness of a nation depended on its dominion over the world's seaborne trade routes. Could America shirk the challenge of becoming great, of fulfilling her destiny, and of establishing democracy's supremacy on the waves? The book was enormously popular with young intellectuals like Henry Cabot Lodge, a future Senator from Massachusetts and Republican party leader, and Theodore Roosevelt, a New York socialite, state legislator, reformer, writer, athlete, and investor in cattle ranches.

The preceding discussion is not intended to suggest that the quest for overseas markets and profits was the primary element in a dawning American globalism that climaxed in 1898. This interpretation has long been discredited in American historical thinking. But equally obsolete is a myth which maintains that America was "isolated" from 1865 to 1898 and then leaped unexpectedly into the arena of expansion as a curious by-product of interest in the Cuban revolution of 1897 and the goadings of "yellow journalism." The fact seems to be that the nation was on the move in all directions.

Whether the missionary and the battleship were only the agencies of the countinghouse—whether the flag preceded or followed the dollar sign into Asia and Latin America—is not a valid question. The flag, the cross, and the dollar sign were part of a trinity of symbols vital to late nineteenth century America. The quest for expansion was "economic" in the sense that Jacksonian democracy, the Civil War and Reconstruction, and the settlement of the West were "economic." All strived for an enlargement of the nation's planting, trading, and manufacturing activities in the belief that these activities fostered and validated American ideals, that they nourished progress. Liberty and prosperity were, together with the Union, one and inseparable.

Therefore, it was to the greater glory of "triumphant democracy" (the title of a thoroughly optimistic book of 1886 by Andrew Carnegie) that businessmen filled emptinesses with steel rails, raised factories, removed Indians, scraped mountains hollow, and denuded hillsides of timber. Henry Adams tried to reduce history to a series of physical formulas. Although his equations were arbitrary, it is nevertheless possible to perceive in the rush to the West, in the industrialization of the South, and in the beginnings of world-wide commercial penetration, the energies of dispersal at work—as formidable as the energies of concentration visible in urbanism.

The nation was prospering through the release of these energies. The prosperity, however, was not uniformly distributed. Other developments of the period, among them labor strife, racial unrest, and agricultural depression, were traceable to the fortunes of certain groups who were "outsiders" in the feast of expansion.

Chapter V

A New American Population (1870–1910)

In one sense, the Civil War was a struggle to determine whether there was a single American people instead of "the people of the several states." The affirmative answer was registered at Appomattox Courthouse on April 9, 1865. Yet this national populace, whose political existence was guaranteed by the war, began to change irrevocably after 1865. Before then, it was a relatively stable group of people much alike in wealth, calling, and beliefs, who lived primarily in rural areas. As postwar years went by, the populace changed into an interdependent mass of men and women of varied backgrounds—largely city dwellers and industrial workers. New occupational and social groups came into being, and had to find fresh ways of dealing with each other. Moreover, the Jacksonian ideals of equality and individualism were hard to apply in such an enlarged and altered nation. The social struggles of the period from 1870 to 1914 partly reflected the difficulty of the task.

OUTSIDERS AND OLD VALUES

We have already seen evidence of the tidal pull of the city on rural folk. The economic changes associated with this migration from the farm are clearly shown by census statistics. In 1860, out a gainfully employed population of about ten and a half million, approximately six and one quarter million were involved in farm occupations as opposed to trade, industry, transportation, and the professions. By 1880, a work force of seventeen million was almost equally divided—eight and one half million in farming, and a similar number otherwise employed. By 1890, however, persons who worked in agriculture numbered ten out of twenty-three million, and in 1910 fewer than thirty percent of about twenty-six million working

Americans were on farms. More than half the nonfarm workers in 1910 were engaged in mining, manufacturing, construction, transportation, and public utilities. In less than a lifetime, we had become a nation of industrial workers instead of a nation of farmers.

We became also a nation of noticeable newcomers. The word "noticeable" is important to bear in mind. Total annual immigration to the United States after the Civil War rose from a quarter of a million in 1865 to peaks of nearly 800,000 in 1882 and a million in 1905, with occasional declines, especially in depression years (see Figure 1). A high point was established with 1,285,349 immigrants in 1907 and, by 1910, the total number of foreign-born in the country was fourteen million—with another nineteen million of "foreign or mixed parentage." These fourteen million foreign-born were 14.5 percent of the total American population. But in 1860 the country's four million "nonnative" residents constituted about 13.2 percent of the total population. Thus, despite popular assumptions to the contrary then and since, there was no striking change in the total proportion of the foreign-born. There was, however, a dramatic change in the visibility of the "alien" because of a change in the sources of immigration and the

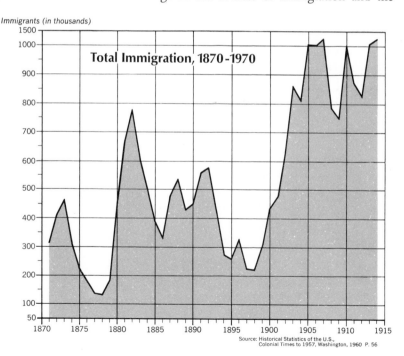

Immigrants (in thousands)

Total Immigration, 1870-1970

Source: Historical Statistics of the U.S.,
Colonial Times to 1957, Washington, 1960 P. 56

occupations available to recent arrivals. Until the 1890s, immigrants from the British Isles, Germany, Scandinavia, Switzerland, and Holland made up more than 85 percent of the total. But the great surge of immigration, from 1896 to 1914, consisted mainly of newcomers from Austria, Hungary, Italy, Russia, Greece, Rumania, and Turkey. A large proportion of them, moreover, found their way into mines, mills, and factories. In twenty-one industries studied by a Congressional commission in 1910, nearly 60 percent of all employees were foreign-born, and two-thirds of these were from the countries of Southern and Eastern Europe. What a native American was apt to see when he confronted the "foreigner," in that year, was an urban lower-class wage earner from a cultural background entirely different from that of his own parents and grandparents. The incoming German, Norwegian, or Irishman found communities where his own kind had been known for a generation or more: the Sicilian, the Greek, the Pole, or the Magyar was doubly a stranger.

In a sense, too, the four million freedmen of 1865, whose numbers had increased to just under ten million by 1910, were also newcomers. True, the first Negroes had landed in Virginia in 1619, the year before the *Mayflower* arrived off Cape Cod but, as independent members of society, the ex-slaves and their children were as inexperienced and even more handicapped than immigrants just down the gangplank.

These sweeping changes in the composition and activity of the populace were creating a new social order. Yet it was one still officially guided by the expectations of an earlier era. In a youthful America, social thought dealt with a few basic figures: the yeoman, the artisan, the merchant, the professional man. Their self-sufficiency and ambition were the cornerstones of American democracy. Their freely chosen government spared them burdensome regulations and taxations, educated them, and encouraged them to pursue their self-interest. As the nation grew, so did their opportunities. Proof of success was in the ownership or enlargement of productive property. This was the goal of all laudable effort and the proof of respectability. Abraham Lincoln explained it to a Wisconsin agricultural-fair audience on the eve of the Civil War as he defined and glorified "free labor." The "prudent, penniless beginner," he said, worked for another for a time, accumulated a competency, then became an owner who toiled on his own account, and perhaps employed others on the way up. "If any continue in the condition of a hired laborer for life," Lincoln continued, "it is because of a dependent nature which prefers it, or singular folly or improvidence or misfortune."

The vision was keyed to the old Puritan virtues of hard work, hard study, and advancement. Yet, in deifying growth, the vision also encouraged speculative investment and capital risk. In the quest for economically fruitful ventures, many respectable nineteenth-century Americans (who would not have borrowed a dime for personal expenditures) did not hesitate to go deeply into debt in order to invest in lands, banks, canals, and business ventures of every kind. Their hopes of success glowed brightly, no matter how far-fetched the project. This was not considered as gambling but as contributing to progress. Faith in progress legitimized the crapshooter lurking in the heart of every respectable citizen who laid out a spare dollar in land or stock purchases.

Such was the dream that formed the substance of a confident young nation's outlook on life. It was one of the forces that energized people who, for the most part, had access (or legitimate hope of access) to the means of genuine economic independence—land, professional learning, and income-generating property. But the new America of the 1880s and 1890s was full of people for whom the old promises did not hold true. The industrial worker could not hope to own the vast machinery that employed him, no matter how much he shunned improvidence and folly. The newly arrived immigrant could scarcely enter the race of life advantageously with nothing available to him but an unskilled job and a tenement flat. Self-improvement was equally difficult for the ultimate outsider—the Negro—whom Reconstruction's philanthropy left jobless and landless, twice cursed with blackness and poverty. Even the landowning, staple-crop farmer found success to be elusive. He was caught in an impersonal market system; he was made dependent on others who furnished him with machinery and transportation; and he was reduced from a "noble yeoman" to a self-employed laborer on a heavily mortgaged farm with no prospect of change in sight.

These new personages of social reality wanted to live by the code of diligent advancement which, by 1880, was national orthodoxy. Yet they could not, and consequently were condemned by the already-arrived as if they *would* not.

THE IMMIGRANT: PROBLEM OR PROMISE?

In the half century that followed the Civil War, nearly twenty-five million people moved to the United States, a number equal to the entire population of the trans-Mississippi west in 1910. They came as a part of a general

The faces and postures of these immigrants of 1902 show the mixture of curiosity, expectation, anxiety and resignation that moved millions to make the crossing to the New World.

migration of Europeans to all corners of the world, set on their way by powerful and fateful forces of industrialism and nationalism. These forces had arisen first in Northern and Western Europe, and the first flow of migration, begun long before the war, brought Germans, Scandinavians, and peoples of the British Isles. The same railroads and steamships which brought competing products that drove the foreigner from his tiny farm or his workbench stood ready to carry him cheaply to a new life in the seaboard cities or in the midwestern valleys. For many years, the Germans continued to settle along the Great Lakes and the Ohio and Mississippi rivers, and especially in the fast-growing centers of commerce and industry—Cincinnati, St. Louis, Milwaukee, and Chicago. Swedes and Norwegians settled heavily in the northern Great Plains and engaged largely in farming. Finnish, Welsh, Irish, and Scottish laborers felled trees, mined copper, and laid track in both the old and the new Northwest.

The Greek, Italian, Hungarian, Polish, Serbian, and Rumanian immigrants arrived at the end of the century, when the economic and national readjustments of the modern age began to exert their uprooting energies in Italy, Austria-Hungary, Russia, and the Balkans. These immigrants found a new kind of America. Choice farmland was less available for the taking. The bulk of labor demand was in low-paying city jobs in domestic service or in unskilled occupations in factories or on construction gangs. Inevitably, the most recent newcomers clustered at the foot of the social ladder.

They arrived at precisely the time when thinking Americans were profoundly disturbed by the very existence of urban poverty and were tempted to find scapegoats on whom to blame its unavoidable problems. For some Americans, the recent immigrant was this kind of scapegoat. A still-living legend began to take shape, (1) of an "old" immigration of substantial families who brought with them savings, skills, willingness to work, and a desire to share in community responsibilities; and (2) of a "new" immigration of families, predominantly illiterate and untrained, willing to work for a pittance and live in animal squalor, complaisantly delivering votes to the "boss," crowding the jails and almshouses, and clinging tenaciously to alien communities and folkways, in indifference (if not hostility) to national institutions. Since the "new" immigrants were overwhelmingly from unfamiliar ethnic stocks, it was possible to reinforce them with the testimony of a misinterpreted Darwinism, which held that these characteristics were not the stigmata of poverty but were bred in the cells by the unalterable machinery of genetics. They were, in short, "beaten races."

Like all stereotypes, this molding of the immigrants cruelly ignored exceptions. The Italian fruit peddler and the Polish coal heaver were flaunted as evidence that these groups were attracted by the basest callings, but the Italians who grew vines in California, or the Poles who bought abandoned Connecticut farms and became truck gardeners were overlooked. The Czech glassblower who could read two languages—German and his own—was denounced as an "illiterate" along with the genuinely unlettered Croatian steel puddler. The successfully Americanized Jewish clothing-store owner was forgotten by opponents of immigration who worried about the assimilation of the Lithuanian sweatshop garment maker, in flight from Russian anti-Semitism, who slept on rags in a basement. The millions of immigrants whose hopes for themselves and their children were to achieve middle-class style were branded as dangerous when a foreign-born anarchist or Socialist hit the headlines. Critics muted the whole contribution of foreign-born intellectuals to national arts, letters, and scientific endeavor, and the contribution of immigrant workers to building the economy.

The post-1890 immigrants did behave in ways that were novel to American experience but that were clearly dictated by their environment. They clustered in ethnic neighborhoods of pronounced "foreign" flavor, partly to ease the shock of transplantation. If some of these neighborhoods were slums, it was a natural result of the fact that the newcomers could afford only the lowest rents. The alliance between the immigrant and the boss rested on the machine's forthright offer of direct help to the new voter with his bread-and-butter problems. If anything was needed to prove that the "alien's" life style was a matter of response to his needs rather than his heredity, it was the speed with which the new immigrants and their children, once they achieved an improvement in status and income, tended to abandon their "old-country" clubs, newspapers, neighborhoods, churches, and political leaders.

This kind of defense of the immigrant's supposed strangeness would not have impressed a growing group of advocates of immigration restriction, who gathered strength in the 1890s. They were drawn from several sources. A traditional rural anti-Catholicism motivated the American Protective Association, which was founded at Clinton, Iowa, in 1887. Although the Association faded after reaching a peak membership of half a million in 1894, its task was taken up in 1915 by a revived Ku Klux Klan. A second restrictionist element was furnished by old-stock Americans of good family, who resented the vulgarity and corruption that they saw as characteristic of the new America, and blamed the immigrant for much of it. An Immigration Restriction League, founded in the depression year of 1894, included such distinguished New Englanders as the historian John Fiske, the economist Francis A. Walker, and Senator Henry Cabot Lodge. Their sense of loss and fear was expressed by Henry Adams when he wrote of himself that his world was dead, and "Not a Polish Jew fresh from Warsaw or Cracow . . . but had a keener instinct, and intenser energy[to survive in a competitive, acquisitive society] and a freer hand than he." Fear was also the strongest motive behind a third group favoring restriction: organized labor. Unionists considered the immigrant as a competitor for jobs and a threat to wage standards, even though immigrants themselves joined locals when opportunity offered, and formed a significant part of the membership of unions such as those of the cigarmakers, the garment workers, and the coal miners. The charge that the immigrant was a "pauper laborer" was aimed particularly at Asian immigrants, and an early outburst of working-class restrictionism took place in 1878 in California, where a Workingmen's Party won a number of offices on a platform including an end to the admission of Chinese to the United States. (It seems ironic that the thrifty, hardworking, clean, and education-hungry Chinese and Japanese, who conformed to the canons of the Calvinistic ethic better than most "old immigrants" and native Americans, should have been hardest hit, but bigotry knows no logic.)

The federal government responded to pressures of restrictionism with a series of acts. Chinese immigrants were excluded from the United States in 1882. Laborers, imported under contract, were banned in 1885. Various bills before Congress, prior to 1915, proposed the exclusion of paupers, victims of particular diseases, known criminals, prostitutes, "undesirables," and illiterates. Some of these provisions became law, but literacy tests were defeated by Taft and Wilson with presidential vetoes. Nevertheless the trend was toward the closed door. A diplomatic "gentlemen's agreement" of 1907 barred almost all further Japanese immigration while, in 1910, the congressionally appointed Dillingham Commission embodied the theory of the "unassimilable new immigration" in a lengthy report. Fourteen years later, Congress approved a National Origins Act limiting total immigration and setting rigid quotas on the admission of Southern and Eastern Europeans.

However, even as the restrictionists gained momentum, millions of the new immigrants were actually becoming assimilated, and were replacing their native traditions and outlooks with American ideas of what constituted success and good citizenship. This was most evident among the immigrant youngsters in the schoolyards, who enthusiastically embraced all things American from Plymouth Rock to baseball. "Go to the public school," a reporter counseled the fearful immigrants, "and hear the children speak the tongue that is sweet to your ear; hear their young voices as they salute the flag that is *theirs*." In fact, the Americanizing process was so thorough that some social critics later lamented that it destroyed the possibilities of a rich, multinational culture. It is likely, however, that the average immigrant of 1910 was quite willing to be entirely loyal to the American way in all things, if given permission.

The potent Americanizing force, the schoolroom, is shown here in its rundown grandeur—including unshaded windows, bare steam pipes, hard seats and attentive scholars. You can almost feel the concentration.

The resistance to granting this permission was a part of the difficulty in stretching the ideal of opportunity for all to fit new circumstances. The inconsistency of nativism was wryly caricatured by "Mr. Dooley," Finley Peter Dunne's make-believe Irish bartender:

> . . . As a pilgrim father that missed the first boats, I must raise me claryon voice again' th' invasion iv this fair land and be the paupers an' arnychists iv effete Europe. Ye bet I must—because I'm here first. . . . Me frind Shaughnessy says. . . 'Tis time we done something to make th' immigration laws sthronger' says he. . . . 'But what ar-re th' immygrants doin' that's roonous to us?' I says. 'Well,' says he . . . they don't assymilate with th' counthry,' he says. 'Maybe th' counthry's digestion has gone wrong fr'm too much rich food,' says I' 'perhaps now if we'd lave off thryin' to digest Rockyfellar an' thry a simple diet like Schwartzmeister, we wudden't feel th' effects iv our vittels,' I says. "maybe if we'd season th' immygrants a little or cook thim thurly, they'd go down betther,' I says.

THE YEOMAN IN TROUBLE

To call the farmer an "outsider" in American life appears, on the surface, to be a misnomer. He had been praised by generations of orators as the backbone of society, and the Republican party had won in 1860 with the promise that the public domain should be free soil, reserved for him against the competition of slavery. The Homestead Act of 1862, bestowing a free 160 acres on any citizen who would cultivate them, seemed to fulfill that promise, and to many farming Americans this, rather than the freeing of the Negro, was the Republicans' finest achievement.

But the wholly independent farmer, dwelling on his own soil, afraid of no man, was a figure of a fading past. New farm machines and the railroad enabled him to grow and sell far more produce with the same investment of labor. These blessings enabled him to specialize in the production of market crops without diverting his energies (as his grandfather did) to hunting for his food and to making his own clothes and furniture. But, simultaneously, these blessings of progress reduced the number of farmers and involved him tightly in the web of large-scale capitalistic production and exchange, at great cost to his autonomy.

Even the well-off Plains farmers (like the Rawding family of Nebraska shown here) lived a life of basic austerity. The sod house (complete with rooftop cow) was minimal shelter in a bare environment. The Rawdings (and the horses) look undaunted, however.

The effect of the railroad on the Eastern farmer was an example of the mixed benefits brought about by technology to agriculture. The roads helped the farm owner of New England or of the mid-Atlantic states to reach urban markets, and to share in the benefits of cheaply transported, mass-produced consumer goods. But the railroads also flooded Eastern markets with cheaply grown western wheat and corn. The farmers of the East, hard-pressed by such competition, were driven more and more into specialized agriculture, such as dairying, poultry raising, and the production of hay, oats, rye, fruits, and vegetables. This transformation of Eastern farming, which began in the canal era of the 1840s, eventually involved many of the farms of the "Old Northwest," of Ohio, Indiana, Illinois, Michigan, and Wisconsin.

However, specialized farm operations required heavy outlays of capital for breeding stock and buying fertilizer, special feeds, barns, coops, and a variety of machines developed between 1880 and 1910: pickers, shellers, sprayers, cultivators, automatic rakes, binders, and presses. Moreover, worn-out soils, labor scarcity because of migration away from the countryside, unusual plant and animal diseases, and changes in public taste combined to make farming especially hazardous for the producer of foodstuffs in the older regions of the nation.

The farmers who could not reduce unit costs of production were squeezed out as readily as their counterparts in small business. Land values sank, farms were abandoned, and in parts of the rural East the sturdy yeomen became impoverished "natives," working for summer vacationers. The railroad, which freed the farmer from wearing homespun and burning homemade tallow candles, helped to transmute him into an unsuccessful businessman in a backwater. The rural village also felt the pinch of economic failure, and the farmer who got second-rate services, whose children received an inadequate education in the pinchpenny country school, who was no longer elected in significant numbers to the legislature, and who lacked electricity, plumbing, and credit, became a travesty of the Jeffersonian idyl.

Yet the Eastern farmer was fortunate compared to the Southern farmer and, in some ways, he was better off than the farmer in the Mississippi Valley and the states immediately to the west of it. This happened for several reasons. The Homestead Act, for one thing, had not built the "New Jerusalem." Much of the best land in the West was included in grants to the railroads or to the states for educational and other purposes, and had to be bought. Many prime areas were preempted by ranchers, lumbermen, and mining companies, often in violation of the Homestead Act. The "free

Land Entries in Selected Years
In thousands of acres

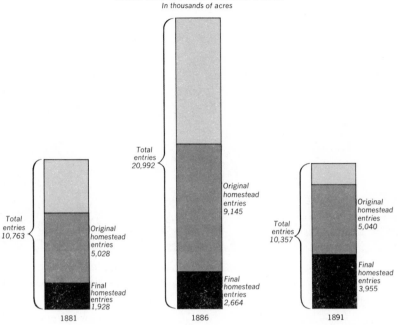

Source: Historical Statistics of the U.S.,
Colonial Times to 1957, Washington, 1960 P. 237

farm" was, by no means, readily available. For example, original entries under the act—that is, statements of intention to work a selected tract—totaled about five million acres in 1881, nine million in 1886 and five million again in 1891 (See Figure 2). But the totals of *all* original entries on the public domain for the same years were ten and three-quarter million acres in 1881, nearly twenty-one million in 1886, and ten and one-third million in 1891. The number of final Homestead Act entries for the same years was far smaller; two million (1881), slightly better than two and a half million (1886), and just under four million (1891). In short, only half (or less) of the public domain, and probably not the best half, was being given away. Capital was still needed to buy a farm, and was usually secured by going into debt.

The prairie farmer was even more dependent than the Easterner on new mechanical and factory-made products such as barbed wire, steel plows, threshers, and harvesters for the conquest of a difficult environment. (The total national value of farm implements and machinery jumped from 152 million dollars in 1850 to a billion and a quarter dollars in 1910.) In areas

Harvesting and other machines, combined with huge acreages, made successful modern farming a big-time operation, as this photograph of a trio of McCormick combines working a vast and vacant field shows.

of little rainfall west of the 100th meridian, irrigation equipment was helpful if not essential, but the 160-acre farmstead was too small a unit to repay the investment that was required or, indeed, to underwrite any kind of large-scale cultivation.

The Western farmer was also especially dependent on the railroads, whose managers did not hesitate to exploit that fact. For example, it was a familiar practice for a road to cut rates in areas of heavy competitive traffic, but to charge exorbitantly for carrying identical goods along lightly populated routes where it had a monopoly. This discrimination among customers was within the bounds of business ethics, but it was hard to reconcile with the railroads' legal role as a "common carrier."

Indignation against arbitrary and unjust railroad rates ran high in agricultural regions. A popular organization of farmers (the National Grange of Patrons of Husbandry) played an important role in the 1870s in securing the passage of state laws regulating railroad charges in Illinois, Wisconsin, Iowa, and Minnesota. However, much pressure for control of transportation rates also came from urban shippers and other businessmen. The Supreme Court upheld these so-called Granger laws in 1877 in *Munn v. Illinois,* but nine years later reversed itself in the Wabash case and denied any state power to regulate interstate commerce. The result was the passage by Congress in 1887 of the Interstate Commerce Act, which provided for federal regulation. Thus, agrarian discontent was partly responsible for a historic first step in national supervision of the economy. Yet federal regulation was ineffective initially, and farmers continued to feel themselves at the mercy of railroad policymakers until early in the twentieth century.

The farmer also resented what he considered as sharp practices by the merchants who graded and bought his grain, and the bankers who lent him money for his operations. Nature also seemed at times to conspire with yeoman's enemies, as droughts, hail, and locusts wiped out crops in a few weeks or hours that represented a year's heavy labor. A bumper harvest, on the other hand, sometimes depressed prices severely, as did other factors beyond the farmer's influence: speculative buying and selling by traders, changes in the volume of bank credit available nationally, and fluctuations in world supply and demand. Essentially the farmer suffered from the fact that he was one of an army of small, competing producers, unable to control very easily the cost, quantity, or time of sale of what he grew. He lacked the key elements of success in a highly organized economy. But he did not always see his problem in these large terms. He was simply and painfully aware that in 1888 it took 174 bushels of wheat to pay the interest on a two-thousand-dollar mortgage at eight percent, with wheat at ninety-two cents a bushel, and 320 bushels to pay the same interest in 1895 with the price of wheat at fifty cents a bushel.

The bitter isolation of prairie life sank the iron deeper into the soul of the farmer who lived there. He was unable to see anything but debt and drudgery in his own and his children's future, and the injustice stung more deeply because he believed, as an article of faith, that he alone produced "natural" wealth, while those who transported, processed, and sold his crops were parasitic middlemen. He looked for an explanation and a cure for the monetary system, suspecting that if currency and credit were more available, rising prices would solve many of his problems. The fundamental grievance, however, was not purely a matter of dollars received. It was expressed by a British newspaper, which noted that in all rapidly industrializing nations, "the agriculturists . . . are becoming fiercely discontented, [and] declare they gained less by civilization than the rest of the community."

The American farmer fitted this description. Civilization had enabled him to produce more, with less brute effort, and to live more comfortably than most of the world's other "agriculturists." Yet business and professional men seemed to be succeeding more spectacularly in the new America, and the rush of progress left the farmer behind the middle-class urbanite in status as well as income. It was not enough to survive. American values demanded success. A farm populace without prospects of success was a new and disturbing element in society.

THE BLACK BOTTOM RAIL: THE NEGRO

The depression-stricken farmer was a fallen hero of the myth that blended agriculture and virtue into one. The post-Reconstruction Negro was in a different situation. He supposedly had no way to go but upwards from slavery. Yet he, too, was doomed to disappoint the expectations of his "friends," the molders of Radical Reconstruction. They believed that, since the ninety percent of the nation's Negroes who lived in the South in 1877 had been given freedom, the ballot, and access to public education, the keys to self-improvement were in their hands. By that year, therefore, even most Republicans believed that the nation might withdraw the protection it had extended the freedmen since the war's end.

Unfortunately, these genial assumptions were untrue. To begin with, Negroes were left without the primary foundation of self-help: economic security. The Radicalism of the late 1860s stopped short of legislating Thaddeus Stevens' suggestion that land expropriated from "rebel" planters be given to the freedmen. Few Negroes, moreover, possessed the means to occupy federal public lands in the South reserved for homesteaders between 1866 and 1876. Nor were most Negroes able to bid for lands that went under the auctioneer's hammer for tax delinquency. The result was that of all Negroes living on farms in 1900, three out of four were tenants—and only 192,993 of the country's eight million Negroes at that date owned farm homes. As a sharecropper or cash renter, the Negro farmer was even more vulnerable to exploitation by merchants and lenders than his white counterparts. Attempts to stimulate Negro migration from the South, like the efforts that sent about 40,000 people to Kansas in 1879, failed because money donated for land purchases, tools, seed, and stock was too scarce.

As a worker, the Negro found that both industry and organized labor tended to bar the door to him. Negroes worked at many skilled trades in the South. They were carpenters, bricklayers, plasterers, plumbers, barbers, painters, and other things. Attempts to unionize them, however, fell afoul of racial prejudice. The national labor organizations of the period (see p. 91) generally considered the Negroes as competitors for jobs instead of additions to the ranks. A National Labor Union, founded in 1866, successfully urged Negroes to form an all-Negro counterpart organization. The Knights of Labor, dating from 1869, more aggressively recruited and integrated Negroes. In 1886, when its membership had reached a peak of 700,000, perhaps 60,000 were Negroes. But in the 1890s, the American Federation of Labor began to dominate the organized labor movement in America, and it allowed constituent unions to set their own racial policies. Many of them (such as the machinists, boilermakers, plumbers, steamfitters, and shipbuilders) excluded Negroes altogether or kept them in segregated and ineffectual locals.

In 1900, Negro workers belonged to only five out of sixty unions covering the skilled trades. Eighty percent of all unionized Negroes belonged to the miners' and longshoremen's unions, which were essentially organizations of the unskilled. Negroes found only a few unskilled jobs in the burgeoning factories of the new South. They represented less than four percent of the labor force in manufacturing. The black man might swing a pick or a shovel, or fetch, lift, and scrub, but he was not likely to rise to dignity and self-support by the exercise of professional and craft skills. And when this "lowest paid, least appreciated and least organized" of all American laborers failed to feed his family, his womenfolk went to work as domestics. In the first year of the new century, 40.7 percent of Negro women were gainfully employed, in contrast to 16 percent of white women.

Improvement through education was almost impossible. Southern state governments skimped badly on education in general, and the Negro got the leftovers of an offering that was meager to begin with. New Hampshire's Senator Henry Blair tried, in the 1880s, to have Congress provide financial assistance to Southern education from surplus federal revenues, but failed. The few Negroes who managed somehow to prepare themselves for higher education found only a handful of Negro colleges open to them in the South. These were weakly supported by philanthropy and received small amounts of state assistance. Some, like Fisk University in Tennessee, were academically ambitious. Others, like Hampton Institute in Virginia, or Tuskegee Institute in Alabama, were concerned primarily with vocational education and character building. The earnestness of their founders, faculties, and students could not entirely compensate for their serious limitations as nurseries of intellect and professional knowledge.

Nor could the Negro exert political influence in order to remedy his condition. The Fifteenth Amendment was largely unenforced, as Southern whites drove the ex-slaves from the ballot box by means ranging from fraud to violence. Mississippi furnishes an illustration of the gradual but inexorable decline in Negro participation in politics after 1876. In that year, twenty-one Negroes served in the state legislature; in 1890 there were five, and a few Negroes in minor county posts. Thereafter, even such token officeholding fell before an onslaught of white supremacy. Southern states modified their constitutions to allow for election laws with devices such as literacy, taxpaying, and property tests, which could be manipulated to exclude Negroes and admit whites. Another method was "grandfather clauses" that restricted the suffrage to people whose ancestors voted before Reconstruction. And there still other constitutional provisions aimed against black voters. In the forthright words of one South Carolina Senator, "we have scratched our heads to find out how we could eliminate the last one of them." Mississippi led the way with this kind of constitutional revision in 1890, followed by South Carolina, Louisiana, and eventually the other formerly Confederate states. Senator Henry Cabot Lodge of Massachusetts sponsored a measure in 1890 to permit federal supervision of elections where deliberate exclusion of voters was charged. Congress did not pass the bill, however. The nation was still seventy-five years short of once more guaranteeing the Negro a free ballot.

The handicaps of the Negro were compounded by the humiliations of segregation, in which the nation acquiesced. In the Civil Rights cases of 1883, the Supreme Court held that while Negroes were United States citizens entitled to the equal protection of the laws, they were not guaranteed thereby against discrimination by owners of hotels, theaters, and restaurants. In *Plessy v. Ferguson,* in 1895, the highest court affirmed the validity of a Louisiana law requiring "separate but equal" accommodations on railroads. In effect, the two decisions legalized the Jim Crow laws, and nullified most of the Fourteenth Amendment, just as the South was perfecting methods of evading the Fifteenth Amendment.

The Negro was thus hobbled legally, socially, economically, politically, and educationally, yet somehow was supposed to prove his worth by bettering his condition in life, as national expectations dictated. Astonishingly, many Negroes did exactly that. In commenting on the restraints imposed upon Negroes, the historian is in danger of overlooking the race's achievements under difficulty. Negro literacy rose from 20.1 percent in 1870 to 55.5 percent in 1900. Negro churches and religious bodies struck lasting roots in the black community. A small but significant number of Negro businessmen flourished in the soil of oppression, for a paradox of segregation was that it forced Negroes to turn to other Negroes for services, thus encouraging black entrepreneurship. Negro professionals also found opportunities among their own race, as about 1700 Negro physicians, 21,000 teachers, 15,000 clergymen, and 730 lawyers of 1900 proved. Although successful, professional, black men numbered only a few in every hundred, they were a living refutation of the stereotyped belief that the American descendants of Africans were naturally inferior and, in the words of a Southern writer, had "not yet exhibited the qualities of any race which has advanced civilization."

Nevertheless, the overall prospects of the Negro in the United States in the 1890s were thoroughly unpromising. Midway through the decade, a remarkable black leader appeared with a plan for improving them. This was Booker T. Washington. He was born in slavery in Virginia in 1856. As a boy he toiled in a coal mine while acquiring the rudiments of education, and doggedly worked his way through Hampton Institute in the very best tradition of self-made Americans. He was appointed superintendent of Tuskegee Institute in 1881, and was remarkably successful. He became convinced at Tuskegee that the Negro's first need was for economic self-sufficiency, and that the white South, also struggling to escape from regional poverty's grip, might help Negroes to achieve that goal in return for the surrender of claims to immediate political and social rights. In 1895, an invitation to open an exhibit of Negro business achievements at the Cotton States Exposition in Atlanta gave Washington a chance to publicly propose this exchange.

Washington's speech outlined what was soon called "the Atlanta Compromise." To Negroes, he announced that their best hopes lay in cultivating the friendship of their inevitable neighbors, the Southern whites, who were willing to give black men "a man's chance" in the world of commerce. Efforts to prosper in agriculture, industry, and business would bring more certain rewards than agitation for political and social rights which could come only in the wake of economic progress. "The wisest of my race," he said, "understand that the agitation of questions of social equality is the extremest folly and that progress in the enjoyment of all the privileges that will come to us must be the result of severe constant struggle rather than of artificial forcing." To whites, he recommended a reliance upon the potential labor contribution of the Negroes, the "most patient, faithful, law-abiding and unresentful people that the world has seen." Together, white and black Southerners could realize Henry Grady's flourishing, visionary new South—"in all things . . . purely social . . . as separate as the fingers, yet one as the hand in all things essential to mutual progress."

The address was a sensation. The white audience cheered, and the governor of Georgia, flinging custom to the winds, seized the Negro educator's hand and shook it vigorously at the conclusion of the talk. Washington was launched on a career as "official spokesman" for the Negro. He was pictured on the covers of northern magazines, awarded honorary degrees, invited to lunch at the White House by Theodore Roosevelt and, above all, consulted in any project for funneling money into the training of Southern Negroes. He also underwent severe criticism from others of his race, who claimed that he abandoned the Negro's just claim to full citizenship in return for donations to an inherently debasing segregated educational system. Opponents also asserted that his plan for turning more Negroes into small tradesmen and artisans offered no real future to them in a business system dominated by large and powerful organizations. W. E. B. DuBois, a Harvard-educated Negro sociologist, charged that Washington's glorification of hard work and accumulation overlooked the problems and needs of talented and intellectual Negroes, denied the particularly poetic and imaginative qualities of Negro life, and merely aped middle-class white materialism. Washington's defenders claimed, in response, that he only disputed priorities, not goals, with other Negro "liberators," believing that economic opportunity must precede acceptance. This debate is not yet dead in Negro life.

For the student of the late nineteenth century, however, the significance of Washington's program is in its perfect reflection of the faith that the man who prospered by his own labor and achieved propertied status could not fail to be accepted as an equal in society. As a northern newspaper stated in reaction to the Atlanta address:

> He had done more for the improvement of the Negro in the South than has been accomplished by all the political agitators. . . . The possession of a vote does not always insure respect, but the possession of a good character, a good home and a little money reserve always insures respect. . . . If every southern state had such an institution as that at Tuskegee, Alabama, presided over by such a man as Professor Washington, the race question would settle itself in ten years.

Unfortunately, persons who applauded Washington's leadership failed to provide many opportunities for Negroes to enjoy "a good home and a little money reserve." His belief that the chance to earn a dollar in a factory was more valuable in 1895 than the right to spend it in an opera house never was tested because factory doors and opera houses alike remained closed, for the most part, to black wage earners. Yet the enthusiasm with which whites embraced Washington's formula for preserving discrimination and simultaneously reaffirming economic improvement as the highest of goals showed how shrewdly he read the national mind.

THE PERMANENT WAGE EARNER

The political orators who outlined the glories of "free labor" in 1860 assumed that the hired laborer was only temporarily at work for someone else. When the "prudent, penniless beginner," as Lincoln called him, had accumulated a stake, he would emerge from his cocoonlike hireling stage in the butterfly colors of self-employment. Twenty-five years later, however, the scope and speed of large-scale industrialization made it clear that the 1860 script would not be followed. A permanent class of wage earners would be as much a feature of modern life as the factory or the corporation itself, and to this class most Americans who earned their bread would eventually belong. This change in the social expectations of the laborer was in itself a profound source of anxiety and discontent in the "new" post-1877 nation.

Workingmen had more to complain of, however, than the dwindling prospects of their becoming independent capitalists. During the concluding quarter of the century, wage levels as a whole were low. True, evidence shows that they did not usually fall far behind living costs, and occasionally exceeded them. But figures based on overall averages do not adequately reflect the problems of individual workers in depressed areas, or in particular industries at different times. The persistence of demands for wage increases in industrial disputes shows that the laborers themselves in great number placed inadequate pay high on their list of grievances. In an advancing and success-minded country, adequacy meant more than bare subsistence.

However, there were other complaints that are easier to define precisely. The average work day was a long one and, despite all the labor-saving machinery of the age, it shrank only from eleven to ten hours between 1860 and 1890. The replacement of hand skills with machine techniques made it possible for veteran craftsmen to be replaced with lower-paid unskilled workers,

The bent backs of these small boys picking slate out of coal in an unidentified colliery show the terrible reality of the abstract term "child labor" (early twentieth century, photograph by Lewis W. Hine).

including women and children. The physical conditions of industrial labor were repulsive. Employers, involved in fierce competition, were not of a mind to increase their costs by providing sanitary facilities for their factory hands or safety devices on their machines. Above all, the sharp upswings and downturns of the business cycle in an unregulated economy brought to life the worst threat of all: insecurity. Samuel Gompers, as a boy in London, heard idle workmen on the streets crying: "God strike me dead. My wife, my kids want bread and I've no work to do." He was to hear the same lament many times in the America to which he migrated in 1863.

As early as 1866 there were some men who realized that workers in large-scale industry would have to organize (precisely as corporations themselves were organizing in combinations) if they hoped to exert pressure on managers to meet their demands. Leaders of about a dozen national unions of skilled workers—men like William H. Sylvis of the iron molders, John Siney of the anthracite miners, and Richard Trevellick of the ship carpenters—

joined that year in calling a convention, which established the National
Labor Union (NLU). This, presumably, was a first step in the mobilization
of the laboring hosts. The composition and fate of the NLU, however,
illustrated basic difficulties in the way of creating a strong and united
movement. The term "labor" not only described the work of individuals
as diverse in skill as ditch-diggers and diamond-polishers, but was also the
word used for any effort resulting in the production of wealth. Under that
generous definition (widely accepted in the 1860s), farmers, professional men,
and manufacturers were entitled to participate in the task of improving
"labor's" rewards by whatever means seemed to them appropriate.

Therefore, the annual meeting of the NLU attracted not only delegates
from unions but delegates from organizations whose primary interests were
in reform. Advocates of a greenback currency lifted up their voices; cham-
pions of votes for women had their allotted time on the platform; denouncers
of land monopoly and railroad exactions were heard. The wishes of these
rebels went into the declarations issued by the NLU, along with demands
of more direct impact on wage earners: the eight-hour day, restriction of
immigration, or prohibition of manufacturing by convict labor. Despite these,
the predominant note struck by the NLU was that of middle-class idealism.
The NLU's major spokesman looked toward a self-employed work force,
perhaps owning large industries cooperatively, and finding its enemies not
among bosses but in such "unproductive" drones as bankers and middlemen.
Tactically, the leadership frowned on strikes, which interrupted the creation
of goods, and greatly hoped for achievement through political action.

The working classes showed little interest in this kind of program.
Attendance at NLU conventions, especially by delegates from unions, shrank
irretrievably until the organization died in 1872. One of its last acts was
to launch an Independent Labor Reform party, whose presidential candidate
drew an infinitesimal fraction of the total vote. The two major parties had
already divided almost the whole electorate's loyalties between them, and
were quite secure against any assault by labor or other reform politicians.

In 1869 an imaginative organizer named Uriah Stephens created, with
a group of fellow garment-cutters, a secret society that was to be the nucleus
of another nationwide labor organization. Stephens called his clandestine
fraternity the Noble and Holy Order of the Knights of Labor, and endowed
it with a set of mystical rites, symbols, and titles. In doing this, he showed
a shrewd sense of the workingman's psychic needs, for to be a Venerable
Sage or a Worthy Foreman created a more exhilarating self-image than to

work merely as the secretary or the president of Local Sixteen. Although the members were aware of the strife between capital and labor, and worked in secrecy to protect themselves against employer reprisals, they nonetheless subscribed to a set of principles which, like those of the National Labor Union, exalted uninterrupted production and cooperation. Stephens' florid constitution for the Knights actually excluded from the circle of social harmony, and from membership, only the drones of society—bankers, lawyers, and liquor dealers. The demands of the Order included national ownership of railroads, telegraphs, and telephones but, otherwise, were substantially like those of the NLU.

Organizationally, however, the Knights differed from the NLU in a significant respect. The unions that sent delegates to NLU conventions were national bodies of workers in the same calling. But as the knights grew, their local assemblies (usually drawn from a single craft or shop) were grouped *regionally* into district assemblies, which consequently included laborers of various occupations. Representatives of these mixed assemblies came to dominate policymaking in the Order. To an even greater extent than the NLU, therefore, the Knights pursued general reform objectives, on which workingmen of widely different skills and needs could agree.

In 1881, Terence V. Powderly became the General Master Workman, the grandiloquent name for the leader of the Knights. Although trained as a machinist, he was more of a middle-class reformer than a representative of labor. He entered politics as a Greenback candidate for the mayoralty of Scranton, Pennsylvania in 1878 and won three successive terms and, despite the distrust of lawyers expressed by the founder of the Knights, Powderly studied law independently and was admitted to the bar in 1894. He was an advocate of industrial arbitration and cooperatively owned factories. But he was an enemy to alcohol, land speculation, and monopoly. The "reformist" orientation of the Knights' constitution made a man of Powderly's outlook a natural choice as chieftain. He was effective as an educator and debater, and persuaded the Order to abandon secrecy and seek alliances and support among the general public. Partly as a result of this decision, membership grew to a peak of 700,000 in 1886. Part of the increase, however, resulted from the militancy of certain local assemblies which, in effect, functioned as trade unions by presenting demands to employers, and organizing boycotts and strikes (over Powderly's objections). Thousands of restless workingmen were seeking for labor organizations that would operate in precisely this way.

The heirs to labor's urge for collective power, however, were not the Knights but the founders of the American Federation of Labor (AFL), which began its existence in 1881 as the Federation of Organized Trade and Labor Unions. Five years later it reorganized and adopted the name by which it is still known. The genesis of the AFL was in the tribulation of the national unions in the depression years of 1873 to 1877. Many of these unions were seriously weakened by the loss of members, dues, and battles. In the reorganization and housecleaning that often follows institutional crisis, a new breed of leaders began to take over.

The spokesmen for the trade-union movement in the 1880s were well typified by men like Peter J. McGuire, of the carpenters, or Adolph Strasser and Samuel Gompers of the cigarmakers. They were distrustful of utopianism, either as preached by socialists or by white-collar reformers with whom the unions had made an unfruitful alliance in the NLU. Gompers and Strasser were also wary of a militancy that led workmen into premature and poorly financed strikes. As officers in the Cigarmakers International, they provided a system of dues and benefits that made their union a model of financial stability. They also centralized control of the union in such a way as to discourage locals from independent action.

In a sense, these architects of the new unionism were simply applying to the union movement the principles of coordination and advance planning, which were used by the successful giants of the business world. The purpose behind the moves of Strasser and Gompers was to allow the Cigarmakers International executive committee to select a given segment of the industry where a strong demand might succeed, and then permit a local to strike, backed by the full resources of the union, precisely as a business firm might focus on a campaign against a single competitor.

Although they sought economic warfare with the employer, unionists like Gompers and Strasser were willing to confine their efforts to the sphere of wages and working conditions. They were impatient with the pitfalls, compromises, frets, and delays of political involvement, and were especially cool to proposals for sweeping changes such as the abolition of the wage system itself. They accepted its existence, sought to improve cigarmakers' conditions within it, and left it to others to build the New Jerusalem. "We are all practical men," Strasser told a Senate Committee in 1885. "We fight only for immediate objects—objects that can be realized from day to day."

These were the operating principles of the various trade unionists who organized the AFL. They were determined that the basis of a national labor movement should be a set of strong organizations of skilled specialists, each supreme in its own jurisdiction. They wrote a constitution that rigidly preserved that craft autonomy. They were reluctant to embark on broad-gauge social crusades, and they created a structure that guaranteed almost permanently the emergence of leaders who would confine themselves to restricted objectives. The first of these was Gompers, who became the first AFL president and held the office with only one year's interruption until his death in 1924. Fiercely energetic, combative, persuasive and shrewd, Gompers was a magnificent captain. The AFL passed the Knights in membership a few years before 1886 and, by 1904, had nearly a million and three-quarter members enrolled in its ranks while the older organization had virtually ceased to exist.

The triumph of the AFL over the Knights was of lasting impact. The "pure and simple trade unionism" of a Gompers, devoted to the securing of "bread and butter" for workers, superseded the search for social perfection that seemed to characterize the AFL's rival organizations, whether middle-class or Socialist. Although Gompers did not permanently renounce political action by unionists, and although he was certainly idealistic in his own fashion, he did accept the existence of a permanent wage-earning class and of large-scale capitalism as unchangeable features of American life. As a result, he won more than the support of pragmatic unionists. He also secured the toleration of a large element of the American population which had looked upon the very idea of a powerful labor movement with uneasiness.

This was perhaps the most crucial of his victories. Widely publicized acts of violence marked labor's emergence to self-consciousness. In 1877 striking railway workers burned depots and freight cars in Baltimore, Pittsburgh, and St. Louis. In 1886 an unknown hand threw a bomb into a mass meeting in Chicago's Haymarket Square, killing and wounding a number of policemen and bystanders. Three anarchists died on the gallows, wrongfully convicted of that crime. Strikers at the Homestead Plant of the Carnegie Steel Company exchanged murderous gunfire with private detectives and strikebreakers in 1892 and, in 1894, a national railroad strike threatened to paralyze the economy and led to rioting and the occupation by federal troops of Chicago. These and similar episodes deeply touched the anxieties of editors, ministers, legislators, and other social observers who feared that a conflict between capital and labor had begun which could only end in social revolution.

It is ironic that the American urban middle class came to accept Gompers, a firm believer in the strike, rather than Powderly, the spokesman of "harmony" and "cooperation," as the leader to save the country from class war. Yet they did: "bread-and-butter" unionism seemed more in the American grain that a political crusade to universalize justice and progress—a sign of how far the country had come from the days of the founding of the Republican party. This does not mean that the country embraced the AFL with enthusiasm. Labor strife continued into the 1930s with lockouts, court injunctions, and "scabs" freely employed against strikers, amid general national approval. But Gompers, like Booker T. Washington, became an officially recognized spokesman for his "minority" group. In 1903 he was invited to join the National Civic Federation, an organization of "progressive-minded" big businessmen seeking a reconciliation between labor and the corporation, and recognizing in the AFL a practically operated, sound corporation like their own. He was a frequent witness before Congress and a White House guest. He was courted by both parties in 1908, endorsed the Democrats in 1912, and played an important part in getting labor behind the war effort in 1917, as will be shown in the following section.

Like Booker T. Washington, in fact, he was accused of betraying the idealists in his following. The AFL pattern of autonomy for constituent unions of skilled workers left the unskilled at the mercy of the employers. Similarly, the draining away of radical idealism in the union movement contributed greatly to an apathetic rank and file that tolerated corruption on the part of union presidents, as long as the bacon was brought home in the form of benefits. The AFL turned its back on the needs of the Negro and the new immigrant except for token statements of good will and high future hopes.

But Gompers (like Washington) may have made the best bargain attainable at the time. There can be no final answer. By leading a new kind of labor movement that matched the expectations of those who molded twentieth century American public opinion, he had given at least some workers a place in the sun. Moreover, progressive politicians between 1900 and 1916 proved willing to develop an alliance with labor, which bore fruit in laws aimed against some of the more glaring abuses in the industrial system.

Chapter VI

Adjusting Minds to an Age of Machinery

The machine age did not merely change the social and economic behavior of the American people. It forced a revision of their basic ideas concerning themselves and their world, and in all those productions of the mind that expressed these ideas. During the period of 1870 to 1900, American intellectual leaders groped for formulas that would help them adjust to a highly organized society, dependent on complex and powerful machinery and massive mobilization of men and resources to carry on its functions. Such a society threatened to produce feelings of depersonalization and helplessness, as well as huge inequalities in wealth and power. Its very existence challenged traditional American self-confidence and belief that the United States played some special role in a transcendently ordered scheme of things. But thinkers and builders of institutions were able to call upon the very science that was producing the new order and to emerge with a fresh world view. This put (or kept) man, especially American man, at the center of the universe, but as a functioning organism, not a spark of divinity. Modern man was considered as the creation of a God of "progress" rather than the creation of that unchanging and awesome ruler of a fixed universe worshipped by Jonathan Edwards. The nineteenth century saw dynamism, not merely order, as the governing principle of the universe. The handiwork of the Great Architect was never quite complete, and He revealed His messages in ever-changing blueprints. Even secular thinkers called on His name without realizing it and, with rare exceptions, in the fullest confidence that He would answer.

"SOCIAL DARWINISM": THE CATCHALL NAME

The world of post-1870 thought cannot be examined at any point without encountering the name of Charles Darwin. In his book, *The Origin of Species,* published in 1859, he set the capstone on a long period of scientific work in geology, zoology, taxonomy (the classification of living things), paleontology (the study of fossils), and related studies of the earth's form and inhabitants. It was already clear to scientific observers that the planet was ancient, and that it had once sustained plants and animals that were now extinct. Darwin attempted to understand why some species of plants and animals spread themselves over widely scattered areas and multiplied, while others disappeared from the face of the earth. His theory was twofold. First, there was a constant and apparently random proliferation of varieties of animal and plant life. Second, all of these living populations constantly pressed upon their environment to command a limited supply of food. Some succeeded in sustaining themselves and propagating their own kind. Others fell before the challenge of natural enemies. Random variation and natural selection explained the existence of all the diverse forms of earthly life in 1859. What was more, these forms in turn would change as the earth itself aged. The evolutionary process described by Darwin did not exempt that biped mammal who, according to Genesis, was formed by God from the dust. The great English naturalist depicted the children of Adam as successfully adapted primates, especially in his work *The Descent of Man,* published in 1871. Mankind, dressed in its little brief authority, was at least as much ape as angel and the great globe itself was forever in flux.

Not only did this concept revolutionize biological study but, bursting on a western society in the midst of a storm of economic and technical changes, it produced an impact that sent shock waves through every citadel of belief.

"Social Darwinism" is a generic term for the attempt to apply the Darwinian formula for explaining the natural behavior of plants and animals created *with* man to the institutions created *by* man. The very fact that such an effort could be made is one of the most revealing things about late nineteenth-century Western men, who desired a "scientific" rather than a supernatural explanation of their being. The chief artisan of a social philosophy based on Darwin's findings was Herbert Spencer, an Englishman, whose many volumes were widely read on both sides of the Atlantic from the 1870s to the 1890s. John Fiske, a prolific and widely read historian and

Darwin's *Descent of Man* provoked shock, rage and mockery by its suggestions of a common ancestry for men and apes. Here a simian Darwin shows an anthropoid monkey how much they resemble each other.

philosopher, did much to popularize them in the United States. Spencer maintained that nations, laws, governments, churches, families, inventions, economies, customs and beliefs were also constantly changing and adapting themselves to their environment. The individuals who emerged triumphantly in the modern world were destined to their victory by scientific law—evidence of "the survival of the fittest." Whatever stood behind scientific law, if anything, Spencer dismissed as "the unknowable."

A world view of this type was almost tailor-made for acceptance in powerful and "advanced" nations, which thus found their primacy under-written by science itself. In the United States, this view was also attractive to the winners in the social struggles of industrialization. Andrew Carnegie was a profound admirer of Spencer, and wrote a number of pieces designed to illustrate the principle that the steel trust was the inevitable end product of "the law of competition" and that its blessings (in the form of inexpensive steel) were cheaply obtained at the price of a few unsuccessful competitors driven from business. The son of John D. Rockefeller stated the same idea in more humble terms by declaring that the American Beauty rose, in all its splendor, could only be achieved by sacrificing and pruning the little buds that grew up around it. William Graham Sumner, an academic spokesman for the same point of view, denounced any effort to legislate equal-ity between great and small competitors, or rich and poor ones, declaring: "Nature . . . grants her rewards to the fittest . . . without regard to other considerations of any kind. If . . . we take the rewards from those who have done better and give them to those who have done worse . . . [we] shall favor the survival of the unfittest, and we shall accomplish this by destroying lib-erty. . . . Liberty, inequality, survival of the fittest; not liberty, equality, survival of the unfittest. The former carries society forward . . . the latter carries society downwards and favors all its worst members." There, in its full majesty (untempered, in Sumner's writings, by the philanthropy that a Car-negie or a Rockefeller practiced) was the Darwinian justification of an ugly *status quo.*

It is too easy to observe only this aspect of "social Darwinism" and to neglect other aspects. Sumner's pessimism was only one kind of reaction. Implicit in the view of a Carnegie were other possibilities. There was law in the universe. Moreover, there was progress. Through scientific study, man could understand law and anticipate progress. Essentially the system was benign; individuals might suffer in the short run, but the whole human race ultimately benefited from "natural selection." Harmony was in the grand design—which was not very different from what Americans had been saying for two centuries, except that evolution had replaced Jehovah.

But more significant was the effect of "Darwinistic" thinking on many people who were indifferent or even hostile to the arguments of political and economic conservatism in biological dress. For Darwinism carried with it a view of man as a creature of his surroundings. Those surroundings—and man's behavior in response to them—could be studied with the detachment and analytical tools of science. That is the real meaning of social Darwinism. Whether man was but a worm or the pinnacle of the cosmos, whether he was the victim of his environment or could master and manipulate it, he was, in modern eyes, more a creature of matter than of spirit. That was the real reason why organized religion was threatened by Darwinism: not because it upset the Biblical calculations of the earth's age (which had been discredited long before 1859), but because a God who was merely "the Unknowable," or even a God who remained God but worked on humanity through the impact of the environment on man's brain cells, was already beginning to die a little. In order to serve the ends of such a God—if one still believed in Him at all—study and organization counted more than piety and prescribed moral behavior.

THE ORGANIZED APPROACH TO THE ENVIRONMENT

The spirit of the age called for large-scale, coordinated efforts to penetrate the mysteries of nature for human ends. This can best be illustrated by showing these efforts at work in two eminently practical areas—industry and agriculture. But the discoverers who transformed production and communication were not always gifted and lonely dreamers, touched with the spark of divine genius. Increasingly, the process of scientific inquiry was placed on an organized footing. Thomas A. Edison, in the role of an independent tinkerer, began his career of pioneering in the application of electricity to light, sound, and machinery. But, by the 1890s, he had set up an elaborate group of shops and laboratories at Menlo Park, New Jersey, and was assisted by a large staff. Alexander Graham Bell worked out the basic pattern of the telephone on his own, but the development of a telephone network (with switchboards and transmission lines) required many subsidiary inventions, which were produced by teamwork. Electricity, especially, seemed beyond the grasp of the self-financed, solitary researcher. Two of the outstanding theoreticians of electromagnetic phenomena in the century—Charles P. Steinmetz and Nikola Teszla (both immigrants)—performed outstanding work designing generators, transformers, and power grids, backed by the resources of two huge electrical equipment firms: Steinmetz for General Electric, and Teszla for Westinghouse. The initial discoveries in applied science might still be single men's contributions—a point illustrated by the backyard inventors who were successfully working on automobiles in the 1890s. The exploitation of new findings on any scale, however, required money and equipment. The work and power of the mind had to be subdivided and multiplied in order to increase the "production" of scientific knowledge, just as the work of the hand was amplified manyfold in the factory. Methodical exploration of forces largely replaced intuitive guesses. We are still in the midst of this new kind of "scientific revolution."

Farming, too, felt the effects of the new approach to natural forces. In 1862 the national government conferred generous land grants on the states to create or support colleges where agriculture could be studied scientifically, and created the Department of Agriculture. Over the succeeding years the department and the colleges became centers of research in every aspect of crop and live stock production, making possible larger and better harvests grown by farmers who made up an ever-dwindling proportion of the population. This increase in agricultural productivity not only had deep economic and social consequences but was intellectually meaningful in that it displayed the intrusion of the scientific mentality into a business which, traditionally, "the Lord had a good deal to do with." The removal of guesswork from seed selection, soil management, and stock-breeding reduced the sense of awe, of prayerful dependence on nature's caprice, of unpredictability in human affairs. Thus farmers, who, among all the people in the country were most likely to cling to the "old-time religion" on Sunday, were most clearly alienating themselves from its premises on work days.

THE ORGANIZATION OF LEARNING

The process of transmitting society's accumulated stock of experience to the rising generation was also affected by new conceptions of what minds were, and how they worked best. At the level of formal philosophy—of thinking about thinking, as it were—these fresh ideas were well expressed in the movement known as "pragmatism." Its best-known exponent, William

James, was a Harvard professor of psychology, a field of study which he did much to put on a scientific footing. For James, truth was not absolute but was determined by experience. True ideas were "those that we can assimilate, validate, corroborate, and verify." Or, stated another way, truth was known by its works, not by faith. This was interpreted by some critics to mean that values were relative and therefore were easily abandoned for convenience's sake, but this formulation cheapens James's idea. What he did say was that values could only be tested in living them out; that, as life itself changed, they also could and would change. "What meets expediently all the experience in sight," he declared, "won't necessarily meet all farther experiences equally satisfactorily." This still left wide open the question of how to define "expediently," but it was a far cry from cynicism. It was, however, an equally far cry from divine revelation.

Although pragmatism as an organized school of thought may not have had many adherents, its underlying impact was visible in many fields of learning, where the task of the scholar was to find out how men and institutions actually behaved, and not what made up their essence or what unchanging verities they were supposed to reflect. John Dewey, a philosopher and educator born in 1859 (the year of the publication of *The Origin of Species*), clearly perceived the evidence of Darwinism as well as pragmatism in the world of intellect. "In laying hands upon the sacred ark of absolute permanency," he wrote, "[Darwin's ideas had] introduced a mode of thinking that in the end was bound to transform the logic of knowledge." The new scientific investigator did not begin by memorizing general principles, but by asking specific questions about the behavior of matter or organisms under particular conditions. He tested his answers by constant experimentation and observation, and claimed no more than he could prove by that method.

A new kind of higher educational institution was needed to contain such an approach, one in which recitation yielded to research, and the laboratory and seminar overshadowed the lecture hall and the chapel. Graduate study began to come into its own. In the preparation of men for the professions, more time, skill, and effort to foster habits of inquiry were needed, and postcollegiate training in law (often by the method of case analysis) or medicine (with heavy emphasis on clinical observation and experiment) became increasingly necessary to maintain quality. The mastery of an ever-changing body of knowledge demanded more time and effort than did the receipt of the elements of a fixed culture.

Hence, in the period from 1870 to 1900, old colleges were transformed into universities, and new universities were created. Yale gave the first American Ph.D. degree in 1861; Harvard followed not long after and, like many of the better state universities, was soon strengthening its professional schools, introducing innovations such as the seminar, and building laboratories. Cornell (founded in 1868), Johns Hopkins (opened in 1876), Stanford and Chicago (dating from 1892) were all examples of the "new university," heavily emphasizing advanced research in law, medicine, engineering, public administration, and in the "pure" natural, biological, and social sciences. The academic talent hunt for brilliant originators and researchers (which we are still experiencing) got under way, as did the overshadowing of the liberal arts college by the graduate school. The great college presidents were the ones who built the best research faculties, and men such as Harvard's Charles W. Eliot, Cornell's Andrew D. White, Chicago's William Rainey Harper, Michigan's James Burr Angell, or Stanford's David Starr Jordan were the academic counterparts of the "captains of industry" whose corporations dominated various branches of industry.

Professional societies sprang up advocating disciplines that scarcely existed before the Civil War. The American Economic Association was founded in 1885. Its purpose was, frankly, revolutionary in a field long dedicated to preaching the rigorous laws of "classical political economy," since it hoped to encourage the discovery of the way in which markets, prices, rents, incomes, and wages actually behaved under varying circumstances such as, for example, a period of high tariffs or of rapid industrial growth. Its leaders were not backward in declaring that they hoped their findings would bring about social betterment. Between 1880 and 1905, national associations of political scientists, sociologists, and historians were formed, primarily to assist in exchanging the fruits of careful, critical research. The examination of slowly gathered evidence became the dominant business of a well-organized network of scholars trained in the new ways. The expert, or committee of experts, was replacing the philosopher as the symbol of wisdom.

Many of these experts, during the Progressive Period, lent their talents to both the state and national governments when these governments began to deal with problems such as conservation, the control of trusts, or the streamlining of urban administrations. The government and the universities moved toward an ever-tightening partnership. Curiously, the model for this partnership, was found, in the 1880s and 1890s, in the Germany of the Kaiser, where the higher educational system trained an efficient bureaucratic elite in the tasks of public health, welfare, and economic management—but without the moralism or humanitarianism usually associated with American reformers.

The lower ranks of the educational system were also affected by expansion and professionalism. Both the school year and the training period of teachers lengthened, while the school population grew, particularly in the higher grades. In 1870, only 57 percent of the population, between the ages of five and seventeen, was in school, and there were but 16,000 high school graduates. In 1910, 73.5 percent of the five-to-seventeen age group was attending school (about nineteen million in all, overwhelmingly concentrated in the public schools) and there were 156,429 high school graduates. The number of teachers in 1870 was 200,515; in 1910, 523,210. (As an interesting sidelight, as early as 1870 women accounted for sixty percent of that total, and in 1910 about eighty percent. The average year's salary for a teacher in 1870 was $189; forty years later, it was an opulent $485.)

The one-room school, taught by a college student in the three months of winter vacation (when children could be spared from chores), was giving way to the statewide system of educational institutions, including "normal" schools for teacher training. Pedagogy itself was becoming organized around a core of research, and higher degrees in education were being sought and obtained by the hard road of the thesis. The movement known as "progressive education" was also evidence of a new concept of how knowledge was created, acquired, conveyed, and used. In the entire spectrum of education, from kindergarten through graduate school, there was consistent evidence of the new spirit which studied man himself in a rational, organized way—made him the subject of scientific inquiry, as well as its creator.

THE ARTS REFLECT AN AGE OF SCIENCE

Even in the arena of the arts, where the impact of scientific ideas would seem to be remote, the new-spirit environmentalism was felt. It is best shown in the work of certain representative figures in all the arts, and most directly visible in architecture, where aesthetic and engineering design are most closely mated. The dramatic change in late nineteenth century architecture was in the elevation of the urban skyline. The skyscraper was a response to the city's need to create ample working space in confined land areas. Its upward thrust was made possible by new inventions, primarily steel framing and electrical and hydraulic systems that carried people, heat, light, and water to locations several hundred feet in the air. The many-storied office tower was appropriate as a symbol of the age. It reflected and praised scientific achievement, metropolitan energy, and corporate wealth, just as medieval cathedrals paid tribute to God and His angels.

The greatest exponent of a new architecture was Louis Sullivan, whose powerful yet delicate buildings reflected his announced principle that "form follows function." One of his triumphs was the Auditorium Building in Chicago, designed in 1886. Great arches march in bold rows against the entire horizontal façade of the structure to its full height. Heavy blocks of what appears to be natural stone in the walls convey a sense of earthiness that balances their ten-story elevation above the sidewalk. The interior (especially the auditorium), designed for opera, was richly ornamented with figures that were not drawn from the classical vocabulary of nymphs and shepherds but from American life—wheat sheaves, leaves, vines, animal horns, and Indian symbols. Sullivan believed that American structures should reflect the variety, massiveness, and power of the new colossus, and that their beauty should be intrinsic to this theme. At a time when popular architects got handsome fees to design homes for the wealthy which dripped with cupolas, towers, balconies, and varied excrescences, Sullivan's insistence on environ-

Even the rubble of construction material at its base does not hide the boldness and power of Louis Sullivan's Auditorium Building, here shown not quite complete in 1888.

Extravagance in every sense was the hallmark of the architecture commissioned by the rich to display their winnings in the game of enterprise, an example of which is "The Breakers," a Newport mansion belonging to Cornelius Vanderbilt.

World's Fair architecture in 1893 was wildly and uncoordinatedly eclectic, as one can see in this panorama of part of the exposition, showing a Renaissance dome, Roman columns, Romanesque arches, at least one Greek pediment, stone elks and buffaloes, and many other things.

mental integrity cost him commissions but won him the admiration of generations of young craftsmen who trod in his path.

Just as Sullivan demonstrates in architecture the viewpoint that man's environment should be positively reflected in his creative works, Thomas Eakins of Philadelphia illustrates, in his paintings, a new way of visualizing the human creature. Eakins, known for his relentless realism, painstakingly studied anatomy, and was dismissed from an art school position for demonstrating a nude male model to proper young ladies enrolled as students. Paintings such as *The Gross Clinic, Max Schmitt In a Single Scull,* or *William*

"Gross Clinic" by Thomas Eakins vividly illustrates the realism of his work, from the nimbus of hair around the lecturing doctor to the tension-crooked hands of the woman seated at the left.

Rush Carving His Allegory of the Schuylkill virtually live. "Here," the canvas seems to cry out, "are people of real sinew, flesh, bone; their skin crinkles, their joints and muscles bulge; the light catches the shine of their eyes, or stray locks of hair as it would if they stood before you now." Eakins' work is worlds removed not only from the pretty, popular chromos of Currier and Ives but from the leafy solitudes of romantic painters. Other important artists of this period, such as Albert Ryder, Winslow Homer, James Whistler, and Mary Cassatt, produced works in which they experimented "impressionistically" with the effects of light and shadow on the texture of a scene

"Gay Nineties" opulence and gaudiness was not only reflected in such inanimate objects as buildings and furniture. The generous dimensions of Lillian Russell, here depicted, are heroically set off by her thoroughly laced and frogged costume.

or a portrait—sometimes diffusing it over a canvas, sometimes blurring or changing outlines or using unexpected colors in unusual places, but always with the goal of painting what the eye actually *saw,* not what it was expected to see. The reduction of nature to planes, angles, and colored shadows—and men to arrangements of light, dark, line, point, and mass—focused on the world the dissecting and scrutinizing eye of science, but in the service of beauty.

In literature, realism first appears in the pages of a number of writers of the 1870s and 1880s who were known loosely as "local colorists." They painted the peculiarities of regional life with close attention to details such as dialect, costume, folk-memories, diet, worship, and mode of work. Two of the best of these writers were George Washington Cable and Sarah Orne Jewett. Cable specialized in tales of the South, such as those in his well-known collection, *Old Creole Days.* Sarah Orne Jewett, in volumes such as *The Country of the Pointed Firs,* carefully depicted the rugged, unchanging old people of New England coastal and rural communities that were being abandoned. Cable's New Orleans quadroons and French-speaking landowners or Jewett's lobster fishermen and widows of the sea are like the figures of Eakins' or Homer's paintings. They are genuine, and are not abstractions. They respond to the pressures of their inner and outer environments—that is, their character and surroundings—and their fate is written in those surroundings.

Of the better-recalled novelists of the period, modern critics especially admire Henry James, William Dean Howells, and the towering but erratic Mark Twain. The works of James are generally concerned with wealthy Americans and their encounter with Europe. Fearfully involuted in style, their hallmark is a kind of psychological insight that sees people in terms of their inner behavior. This makes James an anticipator of the modern novelist's concern with the "consciousness" of his characters.

Much more straightforward is William Dean Howells. He was born in Ohio, when Martin Van Buren was President of the United States, and lived to see the end of World War I. His innumerable novels deal with American families, usually of the successful middle classes, faced with some social or moral problem. His best-known book, perhaps, *The Rise of Silas Lapham,* tells of a rural New England paint manufacturer's success in business, his unhappy efforts to fit into Boston society, and his final abandonment of a new career because he will not compromise his integrity by a shady deal. What give Howells' novels interest is the fidelity with which he portrays life in the horsehair parlors of post-Appomattox America. His pushy mothers, amiably busy fathers, growing and ambitious children, lawyers, bankers, ministers, and editors are faithful reflections of their surroundings, and behave as they must, being what they are. In certain writers this insistence on the determining force of circumstances was the cornerstone of another school of literature: "naturalism." But while Howells admired and encouraged talented novelists like Hamlin Garland, Frank Norris, and Theodore Dreiser who followed this Darwinistic and foreboding literary mode, he could not give up his own optimism. He deplored the decline of American ideals as he had known them when he was a youthful campaign biographer of Abraham Lincoln, but he remained firm in the faith that "the smiling aspects of life" were characteristic of his country. Consequently, his husband-hunting girls and dutiful young men remain likeable even when thrown into the jungles of social strife. Believing that society's selfishness, not its complexity, was at the root of modern evil, he continued to hope for an awakening of the human heart to love, and rejected a bitter development of his own realism.

Mark Twain eludes easy judgment. His life and work were full of contradictions. He is best known for *Huckleberry Finn* (1885), most of which is an absolute triumph for the naturalistic method—a brilliant rendition of American society in the southern Mississippi Valley about mid-nineteenth century, in all its colors and accents, seen through the candid eyes of an entirely free boy. Yet, Twain would swing from a work of this quality to pot-boiling children's stories like *The Prince and the Pauper* or sentimental historical fantasies like *Personal Recollections of Joan of Arc* (one of his own favorites), as if he could not bear the burden of his own vision.

Born in 1835, Twain's youth was wild; after a stretch as a river pilot, silver miner, and roving newspaperman he hit the literary jackpot with *Innocents Abroad* in 1867 and settled down to a life of respectability in places like Elmira and Hartford. Although he lampooned the materialistic excesses of the new America in books such as *The Gilded Age* (written in collaboration with Charles Dudley Warner), he was constantly scheming to make himself a millionaire by investments in publishing, automatic typesetting, and other ventures. Gadgetry fascinated him. He was sometimes as buoyant as his own creation, Colonel Beriah Sellers, who saw fortune forever just around the corner no matter how seedy his own circumstances. Yet he could fill private journals with dark outpourings of despair over the "damned human race." In *Life on the Mississippi* (1882), he painted an idyllic picture of the spacious life along the river of his boyhood in the first half of the book, and in the second half he enthused over the industrial development of the "new South" which wiped out that world forever—an easy-going world, but resting on the dark sill of slavery.

The best parable of his own life may be in *A Connecticut Yankee in King Arthur's Court* (1889). In it, a Yankee mechanic wakes up in the sixth century A.D. to find that his command of nineteenth-century gadgetry offers him unparalleled opportunities "for a man of knowledge, brains, pluck, and enterprise to sail in and grow up with the country. . . . not a competitor, not a man who wasn't a baby to me in acquirements and capacities." He introduces gunpowder, printing, steam, and electricity to the kingdom, becomes its virtual dictator ("The Boss"), and hopes for mighty progress. But in the end, reaction overwhelms him—superstition and folly, embodied in the church and the nobility, undo his work and destroy him by treachery. Was Twain hinting that man was not good enough to live up to the promise of his own technology? Or was he writing a parable of his own life (dogged by personal misfortune: the early death of his wife and most of his children), whose major tragedy was that his talent came and went fitfully, and left him to the writing of poor burlesques and the delivery of comic lectures to sustain his standard of living? It is hard to say.

However, it is apparent that he was affected by the dilemma of nineteenth-century man who sometimes saw himself both as master and victim of his own engines of progress. And, in the literary and artistic efforts that have been touched on, there was always the evidence of that preoccupation with man as the sum of forces of his environment. This was the link between "Darwinism" and the arts.

CRITICS AND UPLIFTERS: COMMON CONCEPTIONS

The striking thing about most thinkers of the age was their almost universal agreement that the new world of science, materialism, and wealth was (although occasionally frightening), in the long run, full of promise. Even the grimmest conservative "social Darwinists" argued that no matter what burdens might be borne by the losers in the competitive struggle, the human race was the ultimate gainer. Those who challenged opponents of the order which social Darwinists defended were equally at home in the assumption of implicit progress. Critics of the *status quo* did not operate from an aristocratic or orthodox religious basis, which rejected the American promise of happiness for all as a false idol. They argued merely that the promise was as yet unfulfilled, but was within reach of accomplishment.

The churches, as an illustration, generated several responses to the worship of progress and wealth. Some ministers adopted a "Christian evolutionism," which accepted Darwin and what he stood for, and simply proposed that God was constantly refining His handiwork through aeons of time by the process of natural selection. God was, in effect, the author of his own version of progress. Fundamentalists, who still took Genesis literally and were frankly hostile to modernity, gradually came to control less and less of the wealth or influence of their national denominational bodies. Many churchmen, too, when confronted with the social inequities of industrial life, found it easy to believe that victims of the economic system needed only individual, moral uplifting in order to succeed in the game of life. Their representative spokesman was a Baptist minister, college president, and lecturer named Russell Conwell. In a famous and often-repeated lecture, "Acres of Diamonds," he told thousands of listeners, "If you can honestly attain unto riches . . . it is your Christian and godly duty to do so. . . . While we should sympathize with God's poor . . . let us remember there is not a poor person in the United States who was not made poor by his own shortcomings."

This claim was sharply challenged by ministers of the so-called "social gospel" who contended that what industrial society needed was an application of Christian ethics to its very foundations—or, as one of them, Walter Rauschenbusch, put it, "to make over an antiquated and immoral economic system; to get rid of laws, customs, maxims, and philosophies inherited from an evil and despotic past . . . and thus to lay a social foundation on which modern men individually can live and work in a fashion that will not outrage all the better elements in them. Our inherited Christian faith dealt with individuals; our present task deals with society." Rauschenbusch and others like Washington Gladden, W. D. P. Bliss, George Herron, and Graham Taylor actively discussed, in the press and the pulpit, matters such as wages, slums, and the trusts. They also took part in lobbying for welfare legislation, and actively promoted the work of settlement houses and other purely social agencies of reform, even when this created a conflict with their own congregations, many of whom believed that pastors should not try to save the souls of pewholders by assaults upon their income-producing properties. ("Social gospel" preachers were, thus, honorable forerunners of today's activists from the churches in the civil rights and peace movements.)

Yet it is interesting that these men merely wanted Christianity squared with the outlook of reformers who believed in progress. Rauschenbusch asked for a love "so large and intelligent that it will persuade an ignorant people to build a system of waterworks up in the hills, and that will get after the thoughtless farmers who contaminate the brooks with typhoid bacilli, and after the lumber concern that is denuding the watershed of its forests." He wanted Jesus enlisted behind projects of intelligent reform that *could* solve the problems of the day. "Religion," he said, "to have power over an age, must satisfy the highest moral and religious desires of that age." The implication was that the polluted brook and the denuded mountain were not the inevitable products of a materialistic culture, but were the results of a mistaken individualism that would disappear with persuasion. Andrew Carnegie could hardly be more optimistic. The social activists among the ministry were, in a sense, reading collective uplift into God's mind, and this "culture Protestantism" was itself to suffer, in the twentieth century, from the general repudiation of the belief in the automatic improvement of the moral condition of machine-age man.

Also, the intellectual rebels of the academies were not lacking in hopefulness. Lester Frank Ward, in a work entitled *Dynamic Sociology,* called for a study of mankind that would show humanity not simply in combat with environment but in fruitful interaction with it—by invention and adaptation changing it—and, therefore would show man himself, for the better. Edward Arlington Ross, another pioneer sociologist, believed that it was possible, through the study of group behavior, to evolve principles of social change that would form the foundation for a set of scientific ethics. In *Sin and Society* (1907) he tried to demonstrate that individual stockholders in exploitive corporations might be towers of private rectitude but, nonetheless, social sinners. Yet he believed that to recognize this paradox was to take a long step toward solving it. Richard T. Ely, like other modern economists, specialized in economic studies that would replace chaotic competition with planned development, thus eliminating (it was hoped) the suffering caused by panics and depressions. And, as almost every schoolboy does *not* know, the "progressive education" espoused by John Dewey was not intended to free children entirely from school discipline, but to end a slavish adherence to ritualistic learning based on obsolete needs. Dewey believed that man was meant to solve problems, and that his problems were essentially social. Schoolwork should encourage experiment and innovation, and should reward curiosity in order to create individuals who could define and deal with group problems. He wrote, in a pedagogical creed in 1897, that the needs of the child were paramount, but "they must be translated into terms of what they are capable of in the way of social service." The new education, like the new sociology and the new economics, aimed at putting intellect on a "scientific," open-ended, experimental basis, and the conviction dominating the writings in these fields was that research would bear fruit in improved social values. America would not lose its position as "a city on a hill," but would strengthen it.

Popular works that were harshly critical of the national purposes in the 1870s and 1880s were similarly faithful to the idea of progress at the roots. In 1879, *Progress and Poverty* was published. The book was the work of Henry George, a one-time sailor, printer, editor, and self-taught economist who had labored on it for years under what he was convinced was a divine mandate. The opening argument seemed depressing enough: in the midst of vast material progress, want and misery haunted increasing millions. Despair lurked amid plenty. Yet George furiously rejected the idea that such a condition was inexorably dictated by God, or by the Malthusian principle that an expanding population must outrun the food supply, a chief assumption of Darwinism. On the contrary, he argued that the root of the evil was in private monopolization of nature's greatest gift to mankind—the fecund earth itself. As civilization made the soil and other raw resources more valuable, the value of land automatically rose. George asked that society appropriate that increment—which traditionally went (in the form of rent) to owners of the real estate on which progress reared its factories and towns —and release it as working capital for further productive improvements to uplift all men. Although the idea of this "single tax" never won the loyalties of legislative majorities, George's relatively early attack on the chasm between rich and poor, and his insistence on a solution that went beyond encouraging the rich to be benevolent, make him an important social commentator. He had much influence on political progressivism because he was one of the first to announce the heavenly vision of redemption by intelligence.

In 1887 Edward Bellamy's novel, *Looking Backward,* was published. It was considered as protest fiction, and was almost as instantaneous in its popularity as *Uncle Tom's Cabin,* although it was less effective in helping to destroy the evils it denounced. It is the self-told story of Julian West, a young Bostonian, who falls into a deep sleep and awakens in the year 2000. He describes the society into which he had been born as a nightmare of selfishness, a coach pulled constantly uphill by masses of suffering humanity so that a tiny few might ride in idle luxury. But by 2000 that has changed. The government, in a bloodless revolution, has "nationalized" the trusts.

Cooperation has replaced individualism. Work is done voluntarily by members of an "industrial army." All share in the fruits and in the planning, under the leadership of wise and disinterested veterans of toil. Harmony and planning are everywhere, from roofed-over cities with controlled climate to communal kitchens that spare the individual drudgery of hundreds of isolated housewives.

Bellamyite clubs were formed to implement Julian West's dream, but had little visible effect. Bellamy's importance lay in keeping protest alive, and awakening the conscience of the age of limitless acquisition. This was the basic contribution of his followers and of Henry George's single taxers. What is especially revealing, however, is Bellamy's genial certainty that rational planning will make a heaven of the competitive hell. Man is *meant* to prosper through applied wisdom; the modern organization of natural forces on a huge scale, for productive ends, is *not* in itself an enemy to the soul's aspirations, or to the part of the human animal that sees visions and dreams dreams. Bellamy's people of the year 2000 are organized but not regimented; they are economically collectivized but somehow are capable of retaining individual habits, outlooks, and preferences more successfully than their wage-slave ancestors. The society of the future, according to Bellamy, is not a hive of bees without egos, but a community of brothers. History moves unshakably in that direction. And so Bellamy, in the end, was as much a preacher of "triumphant democracy" as Andrew Carnegie.

Yet, in spite of all this optimism, there were alarms and frightening confrontations in the nation. During the 1870s and 1880s the problems described earlier were sharpened and thrust into politics. In the 1890s, a decade of violent storms began, and the faith of the American people in their immunity from agonizing social conflict was severely tested.

Chapter VII

Politics Reflects the Crises (1878–1901)

Between 1878 and 1892, the country's two major parties were more or less deadlocked in contests for national power. In the popular voting for president, the Democrats won in 1876 (only to have the election "stolen"), lost in 1880 by less than 40,000 votes out of about nine million cast, and won in 1884 by less than 30,000 votes out of ten million. In 1888 they beat the Republicans by 90,000 ballots out of eleven million, but lost the White House in the electoral count. Only in 1892 did the Democrats finally get a comfortable margin of 370,000 votes. In only six years between 1875 and 1895 did the same party control the Presidency and both houses of Congress, and in two of those years (1881 to 1883) the Republicans were actually tied in Senate seats with the Democrats, and organized the chamber by getting an independent—Virginia's William Mahone—to vote with them.

Neither party dared to deal with "hot" issues for fear of alienating even small blocs of voters. Victories by such close margins caused the slightest defection in the ranks to be damaging. This was the overriding reason for the apparent superficiality of national politics in this era. Moreover, basic issues did not become sharply visible until the 1890s. Until the issues became apparent, both parties spent their energies in guarding the cohesion of the coalitions on which they rested. The Republicans counted heavily on the Civil War veterans (for whom they were the party of the Union and pensions) and the prairie farmers who identified Republicanism with the Homestead Act. The educated upper and middle classes of New England and the residents of the area of its cultural influence throughout much of the mid-West were loyal to the Republicans as the party of progress and principle. So were the businessmen who were most dependent for growth on government

116

encouragement and protection, and so, naturally, were the Negroes where they still voted.

The Democrats could count on the "solid South" after 1877. They also had islands of strength in some cities with long-established Democratic machines. Moreover, there were farmers and businessmen who derived no benefit from the prevailing Republican economic policies, who turned to the Democrats—as, for example, shippers to whom a high tariff, which reduced imports, meant heavy losses. Generally, the Republicans supported active governmental stimulation of economic growth, and therefore the more ambitious classes of newcomers to industry and agriculture sided with them. Northern Democrats, on the other hand, were inclined, as a rule, to support genuine *laissez-faire* policies, barring not only regulation but assistance to business by government. They scored in sectors of the economy that were threatened by rapid new developments. Individuals tended to align themselves according to their own conception of the economic community to which they belonged. However, local forces, issues, and emotions blurred the

The densely packed, outdoor torchlit rally was a feature of American political life in an urban seeting throughout the last half of the nineteenth century. Here, partisans of Horace Greeley gather in 1872, in a scene that could have been duplicated in many elections.

distinctions between the national parties in contests between Republicans and Democrats for state and local offices. This has made it difficult for historians to generalize about voting patterns, and it was even riskier for contemporary politicians to predict them.

CIVIL SERVICE AND TARIFF: HAYES TO HARRISON

National parties are actually alliances of state organizations. Strong leadership from above or overriding nationwide issues tend to unify them. On the contrary, when a party has neither ideas nor personalities with strong appeal throughout the country, state leaders become more independent and important. The subsidence of Reconstruction's conflicts and the weak presidential role of Grant opened the way in the late 1870s for the domination of the Republican party by state bosses, who controlled armies of supporters by the distribution of patronage. Often, state bosses, such as Pennsylvania's Simon Cameron, Indiana's Oliver Morton, New York's Roscoe Conkling, or Maine's James G. Blaine, made their command post a Senate seat. These men operated like victory-minded professionals. They were seldom demonstrably corrupt but, in awarding jobs and contracts where they would do the most good, they examined party affiliation and personal fidelity more closely than the honesty of the recipients.

The Republicans who were still full of Civil War idealism, and whose outlook remained essentially that of Charles Sumner in the 1850s (when he declared that he was not in politics but in morals), denounced the "spoilsmen" as the authors of corruption under Grant. They demanded reform by replacement of the patronage system of appointments with a corps of civil servants chosen by examination. However, their battle was not, as they viewed it, one of high-minded defenders of democracy arrayed against the hosts of evil. The reformers were rather distrustful of the popular will so carefully courted by the bosses. It was not altogether unfitting that in the 1880s they should be nicknamed Mugwumps, a word of uncertain origin meaning a grand chief or sachem. Their leaders, like Carl Schurz, E. L. Godkin, and George W. Curtis, were more often journalists than practicing officeholders. They lived emotionally in the atmosphere of 1856 and the grand marshalling of the hosts of progress and righteousness symbolized by the birth of Republicanism.

To party regulars, like Roscoe Conkling, talk of ending patronage was the "gush" of "man-milliners, carpet-knights, and *dilettanti* of politics." Parties bound the nation together and achieved practical reforms, and parties were built up by the cement of loyalty—bought, paid for, and delivered. And the "regulars" pointed out that reformers were supported by run-of-the-mill politicians disappointed with their share of the loaves and fishes, and by businessmen who found party infighting expensive, since they often had to finance all contenders to prevent being on the losing side.

The gap between regulars and reformers no longer seems as great as it did to the two groups at the time. Both shared similar views on economic matters and both were reflecting a trend toward specialization. The reformers who desired competence as the key to officeholding were reaching for a "professionalism" of merit. Their "machine" opponents stood for a kind of "professionalism" in winning elections. Both wishes were rather far removed from the Jacksonian idea of fighting an "aristocratic" bureaucracy by frequent rotation in office of amateurs perfectly competent to govern.

Civil service reform was briefly developed in the federal government in the 1870s, and won a well-publicized victory in 1881, when newly inaugurated President James A. Garfield was shot to death by a disappointed office-seeker. Riding the wave of public outrage, Congress the next year passed the Pendleton Act, which set up a Civil Service Commission to select certain categories of federal jobholders by competitive examination. Ironically, the law was signed by Chester A. Arthur, Garfield's successor, a prominent beneficiary of the spoils system.

The tariff question offered greater possibilities than did the civil service question of coming to grips with the issues of wealth, poverty, and opportunity. Denounced as "the mother of trusts," the tariff seemed a fine example of favoritism to manufacturers. Opponents claimed that its reduction would be proof of the national will to equalize opportunity among all the nation's economic groups. Yet the issue was not so simple. The tariff debates of the 1880s almost always accepted two points which had been challenged by an earlier generation of tariff opponents: the constitutionality of protection, and the need for sustaining a high level of manufacturing activity. The fighting then centered on particular schedules rather than general principles, and the deployment of forces became complex. Not only did the tariff produce generous quantities of revenue and even an occasional Treasury surplus, so that there was always pressure to retain certain profitable duties even from enemies of protectionism, but protectionists were divided among themselves. Businessmen and Congressmen who favored high duties on foreign manufactures often enough defended free trade in raw materials. The producers of those raw materials naturally took a stand just the reverse. They wanted competing foreign raw materials excluded, but not manufactured goods from abroad. Although farmers allegedly suffered most from the tariff, growers of crops facing foreign competition (such as sugar and wool) were not averse to a taste of protection.

Therefore, tariff debates broke down into many dogfights, in which men voted inconsistently, blending principle with the demands of their districts, and compromising freely. This kind of "logrolling" was caricatured by Mr. Dooley in the speech of an imaginary Louisiana Senator who denounced the tariff as "a hellish ingine of oppression" against which he would filibuster forever, "onless . . . it is akelly [equally] used t' pr-r-otict th' bland an' beautyful molasses of the state of me birth." The upshot of debates thus enlivened was almost always a raised tariff. Hayes avoided the issue, but under Arthur, in 1882, Congress attempted to reduce the schedules. The result, in one magazine's words, was that "the kaleidoscope has been turned a hair's breadth, and the colors transposed a little, but the component parts are the same." Grover Cleveland, the Democrat elected in 1884 (and again in 1892), made tariff revision a major issue, and supported the Mills Bill of 1887, which called for downward adjustment. The bill died on the Senate floor. The next Congress, which was Republican, returned to the battle, and the resulting McKinley tariff of 1890 was not only protective but even more political than many tariff acts. It reduced certain revenue-producing duties, like that on raw sugar. It compensated domestic sugar producers for this weakening of their protection with a bounty. It sought farm support through introducing the idea of "reciprocity," by granting the President permission to lower the tariff on certain foreign items in return for a reduction of foreign tariffs on American products, especially agricultural commodities. This was designed to help the farmer dispose of his price-depressing surplus. It was a novelty later abandoned. The many-faceted McKinley bill indicated how very complex tariff-making had become, and how difficult it was to define issues clearly through tariff discussion.

THE MONEY QUESTION, 1878–1890—SEEDS OF REVOLT

The money question seemed to come closer to fundamental social conflicts. In elementary form it seemed to be a matter of whether the government should or should not inflate the currency by various devices. Thus it appeared to create a simple division between debtors and creditors. But underlying the debate were deeper themes. In effect, the inflationists were asking that the government should actually undertake to stabilize prices by enlarging the money supply to meet increased business demands in a growing country. (Under the simple quantity theory of money, prices fall when money is scarce *per capita,* and rise when it is plentiful.) The inflationists argued, as William Jennings Bryan was to say in the 1890s, that a dollar approaches honesty as its purchasing power approaches stability: that a borrowed dollar worth a bushel of wheat should be repaid with one that was also worth a bushel of wheat. This was a somewhat sophisticated and modern concept. Yet, in another sense, the inflationists were looking backward. In asking that more currency be pumped into the economy so that credit might be more readily accessible to all, they were also asking the government to keep the paths of opportunity open for the hopeful but poorly financed small investor. He was hardest hit by the growing costs of efficient industrial operation. And it was true that a "hard money" policy, no matter how piously defended in terms of the needs of widows and orphans living on pensions and the proceeds of insurance policies and trust funds, would actually hasten the integration of the economic system by eliminating weak rivals and putting power in the hands of the most heavily capitalized and mechanized corporations, supported by the biggest bankers.

There was consequently a paradox in the debate. The inflationists' "radical demand" for a government-manipulated money supply was designed to save the old order by holding back the price decline that was driving the marginal businessman to the wall. The "conservative" hard-money men, hoping to let "economic law" dictate the money supply, in effect supported a stepping-up of the pace of industrial concentration—the revolution sweeping away the remnants of Jacksonian America.

The issue thus posed, whether or not the antagonists realized it, was one of reaction to modernity. Businessmen and farmers took sides on the question not merely after considering their debts, but in accord with their conscious or unconscious anxieties or hopes concerning the new order. They brought to this battle the tremendous stores of emotion that men always generate when they debate the shape of their future. As a rule, the farmers were the most conspicuous bloc favoring inflation, but some credit-hungry men of industry were on their side and, in 1876, the Presidential candidate of a newly formed Greenback Party was not a farmer—he was old Peter Cooper, a veteran manufacturer, distrustful, as were the Mugwumps, of the pushy ways of the aggressive new business leaders. Labor reformers in the NLU and the Knights of Labor also endorsed "greenbackism," and hopes of a soft-money coalition among small businessmen, laborites, and farmers blossomed briefly but futilely in the late 1870s. Although Peter Cooper received a tiny 80,000 votes in 1876, the Congressional canvass of 1878 yielded nearly a million votes to the Greenbackers. The Greenbackers, united with labor independents in the Greenback Labor party, elected fifteen members of Congress (and many state legislators.) This high-water mark of political greenbackism was primarily a reaction to hard times, but it showed that resentment could breach the ranks of the major parties.

Yet, neither Democrats nor Republicans officially heeded the warning. When Hayes entered office, the country was already committed to "resumption"—that is, recommencement of the payment of interest on its bonds, and redemption of the wartime greenbacks, in gold. These payments had been suspended during the depression beginning in 1873. Hayes gladly endorsed resumption. For him, as for every President after him, the issue was a simple one of credibility. A debt of a dollar in gold bullion was payable with the same dollar, and if this standard was not adhered to, there would be no reason for any lender to put his faith in the promises of his nation, a confidence at the very heart of the money system itself. In fact, the government, if it paid a creditor with a paper dollar worth less than its face value in bullion, connived in his robbery. "Honest money" was as moralistic a slogan as "honest government," and was equally as resistant to precise definition.

But inflationists did achieve one victory in Hayes's administration. In a coinage bill of 1873, Congress had stricken out provisions for the minting of silver coins. The alleged reason, sharply challenged afterward by soft-money forces, was that the Treasury's official price for silver, expressed in units of gold, was unrealistically low. Silver brought more in commercial markets than the Treasury allowed, and hence was not being presented for coinage. But even as this bill was enacted, floods of Western silver were beating down the price, so that whereas in 1872 the bullion in a silver dollar was worth about $1.02 (or was about one-sixteenth as valuable as the same weight of gold), by 1889 it had sunk to seventy-two cents, and was down to fifty cents in 1896. Now the silver mine owners in search of a government-supported market joined the inflationists' ranks creating a curious alliance of millionaires and radicals. They denounced the "Crime of '73," demanded to know what sinister forces had led Congress to strike out the provision for silver coinage merely because it was temporarily inoperative, and called for its restoration. They secured a limited victory—the Bland-Allison Act of 1878, requiring the monthly purchase of two to four million dollars' worth of silver, and its circulation as coin or by certificates representing it. The act had to be repassed over Hayes's veto to become law.

Silver now replaced greenbacks as the hope of the inflationists. The Greenbackers unsuccessfully ran national tickets in 1880 and 1884 on platforms that appealed to labor and antimonopoly sentiment, and steadily declined. In 1884 inflation and economic reform alike suffered a setback when Grover Cleveland was elected. Cleveland, a civil-service reform mayor of Buffalo, then an anti-Tammany governor of New York, was courageous in a negative way. He fought Congress vigorously, and restored strength to a Presidency filled, since April 1865, with second-rate men. But he believed in a frugal and clean government, which meant a policy of no aid to the farmer, laborer, or consumer. The highlight of social reform in Cleveland's first administration was the passage of the Interstate Commerce Act of 1887, setting up the Interstate Commerce Commission to achieve reform of railroad abuses but giving it virtually no power to do the job. Furthermore, in 1890 the Supreme Court bestowed on the railroads almost complete immunity from regulation by asserting that public supervision must not interfere with their right to earn a "reasonable return" to be determined in the courts.

Cleveland therefore pleased political reformers, but achieved little as President to satisfy groups with severe economic problems. His opponent in 1884 was James G. Blaine, the epitome of Republican professionalism, who was widely reputed to have done too many favors for business constituents in Congress. Cleveland owed his victory partly to the fact that Mugwumps, in droves, deserted the party of Lincoln to vote for the more "honest" Democrat.

In 1888, little separated Cleveland and Benjamin Harrison, except the tariff question, and Harrison's election capped an unspectacular campaign. The Congress chosen with him, however, reflected growing surges of discontent. Both Republicans and Democrats had made verbal concessions to antimonopoly and soft-money sentiment in their platforms, and the legislators of 1890 were willing to afford at least symbolic relief. Two acts were passed bearing the name of the aging Senator John Sherman of Ohio. One, the Sherman Anti-Trust Act, was a vaguely worded law making it a federal crime to enter a "combination in restraint of trade." It was aptly characterized by one Congressman as a device to enable the Republicans to go before the country with something labeled "A Bill To Punish Trusts." The other Sherman act of 1890—the Sherman Silver Purchase Act—provided for the purchase of four and a half million ounces of silver per month, to be paid for in certificates redeemable in gold at the option of the holder. The same Congress gave manufacturers the protection of the McKinley tariff, voted fresh pensions for the survivors of the Civil War, and defeated the Blair and Lodge bills designed to help the Negro in the South obtain schooling and the opportunity to vote. But Congress had acted too late. The growing farm and labor distress had fed a discontent that now erupted in a new party. The significant political fact of 1892 was not Cleveland's reelection but a genuine outbreak of rebellion in the backlands. Populism had been born.

POPULISM AND THE ULTIMATE CRISIS, 1892-1896

The farmer, like the laborer, had experimented with association as a remedy for his problems in the 1870s. The Order of the Patrons of Husbandry, founded in 1869 and better known as The Grange, had enrolled thousands of farmers, especially in the Middle West, in its local chapters. Its meetings softened the isolation of farm life and provided a forum for airing mutual discontents. It made efforts to organize cooperative societies for marketing crops and purchasing supplies, and even for manufacturing farm machinery, but the depression of 1873, together with the lack of adequate capital, and experienced, well-connected management, wrecked most of its ventures. In politics the Grange lobbied for state regulation of railroads and achieved some limited success in Iowa, Wisconsin, Illinois, Minnesota, and Michigan (see Chapter V). Its conventions had also endorsed greenbackism. In many ways, including its ritual and its exaltation of "the producer," it resembled the Knights of Labor.

The initial energies of the movement, however, expended themselves and the local lodges (numbering over 20,000 in 1874), in ten years, had dwindled to around 4000. Yet, as farm poverty continued to haunt the South and the great interior basin, farmers spontaneously formed new organizations, known as "Alliances." Many of these organizations were independently founded in both the North and the South and, by 1890, they had coalesced into two great regional bodies: the Northwest Alliance and the Southern Alliance and Farmers' Union. There was also a Colored Farmers' Alliance.

For a brief time it seemed that a union of Southern poor men, which crossed the color line, was possible, but these hopes were soon dashed by white, lower-class prejudice and insecurity. In the end, Southern white Alliancemen, who soon became Populists, responded to racist feeling and joined in the disfranchisement and segregation drives of the 1890s.

Although the Alliances began (like the Grangers) as social and self-help organizations, they moved inexorably toward political articulation of their demands. At first, they tried to capture existing parties. In the South, Alliancemen entered the Democratic primaries, and in South Carolina in the 1880s a movement of Alliancemen, led by a one-eyed, Negro-baiting farm owner named Ben Tillman, captured the state government on a platform of better rural schools and roads, more back-country representation in the legislature, and various direct forms of aid to the farmer. By 1892, when Tillman was elected to the Senate, five Southern states were strongly influenced or controlled by Alliancemen. In the North, the Alliancemen tried various expedients. They backed independent candidacies, often under the labels of "People's" or "People's Independent" tickets. Also they made efforts to take over Republican machinery and, where that failed, they some-times supported fusion with the Democrats. Skirmishes were won by these tactics. In Kansas and Nebraska, in 1890, Alliance-backed candidates won majorities in the lower houses of state legislatures. It soon became clear that major success would depend on national organization. Some agrarian leaders envisioned a political union with the still-active Knights of Labor. Perhaps an army of people in debt and distress might yet march against the citadels of Republicanism and Democracy and overthrow them!

After initial organizational meetings, hundreds of delegates—Alliancemen, single-taxers, greenbackers, socialists, Knights of Labor, and, in one historian's words, "political come-outers of every breed"—gathered at Omaha in July of 1892 to launch the People's (better known as the Populist) party. The full magnitude of the uprising was revealed as the Populists made a series of demands to restore government to the people. The platform began in thunder:

> We meet in the midst of a nation brought to the verge of moral, political, and material ruin. Corruption dominates the ballot-box, the Legislatures, the Congress, and touches even the ermine of the bench. . . . The newspapers are largely subsidized or muzzled, public opinion silenced, business prostrated, homes covered with mortgages, labor impoverished, and the land concentrating in the hands of capitalists. The fruits of the toil of millions are boldly stolen to build

up colossal fortunes for a few, unprecedented in the history of mankind; and the possessors of these, in turn, despise the Republic and endanger liberty. From the same prolific womb of governmental injustice we breed the two great classes—tramps and millionaires.

The remarkable platform then demanded these things: the free and unlimited coinage of silver at a ratio to gold of 16 to 1; a "subtreasury" plan whereby farmers could store their grain and receive loans of circulating notes up to eighty percent of its value; an income tax; government ownership of railroad, telephone, and telegraph lines; the direct election of Senators; the secret ballot; the eight-hour day; and immigration restriction. Most of these planks originated from earlier third-party and protest movements, and some of them had been vaguely echoed by the major parties, but never had such a massive, discordant crescendo of dissatisfaction crashed through American politics. In defense of the restoration of the old American values of equal opportunity for all "producers," the Populists had developed a full-blown radicalism.

The Populists nominated the veteran Greenbacker, James B. Weaver, for President. He received a million popular votes and twenty-two electoral votes from Colorado, Idaho, Kansas, Nevada, and North Dakota. The Populists also elected a number of state officials and congressmen, often in fusion with the Democrats, although joint tickets were very difficult to arrange.

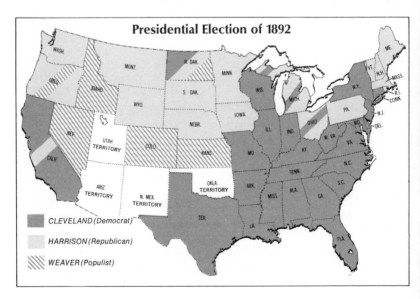

Presidential Election of 1892

CLEVELAND (Democrat)
HARRISON (Republican)
WEAVER (Populist)

The tactic of fusion involved collaboration with long-hated enemies in an age that took politics very seriously. Southern Populists could scarcely relish voting with Republicans (the architects of "black Reconstruction"), and Midwestern Populists were equally ill at ease embracing Democrats, long denounced as "copperheads." Moreover, collaboration invariably involved compromise, and the Populists, like all reform parties, were thus torn between doctrinal purity—staying in "the middle of the road" with independent candidates and making no concessions to the old guard—or combining with other forces and increasing the chances of victory. This dilemma was to cause their undoing in 1896.

Populism shocked and frightened conservatives. They considered it a movement of fanatics and failures and, above all, of irresponsibles who would repudiate the sacred obligations of punctual and honest payment of debts that powered the whole complex circuitry of modern business. The Populists contributed to this stereotype by the impulsiveness of their rhetoric—their pentecostal outbursts of anger at the money-changers in the temple of democracy, and their Cromwellian conviction that God upheld their hands. Some of their leading spokesmen, too, were easy to caricature—for instance, Ignatius Donnelly of Minnesota, writer of radical novels, dabbler in cryptography, and devout exponent of myths such as the lost continent of Atlantis or the authorship of Shakespeare's plays by Bacon; or Mary Ellen Lease, the Kansas "pythoness," a work-hardened farm wife who talked the down-and-outers' own language, urging them to "raise less corn and more HELL!"

But these individuals received considerable attention from a uniformly hostile press because they were easy to lampoon. Behind them stood thousands of perfectly "normal" middle-class American farmers who were at rope's end—they were radicals only out of desperation. Apparently the Populists were so violently denounced because they had broken the consensus of optimism. They had not rejected the American dream of self-sufficiency in favor of "socialism," but they were unwilling to pretend any longer that the dream was working for large segments of the populace. Like the abolitionists (the last wave of "radicals" who preceded them), they were forcing society to look beyond its pretenses, to its actual record. This is the way to earn castigation in American life. Actually, most Populists were only temporary "extremists" and, like most abolitionists who slipped quickly back into political normality once the Thirteenth Amendment was passed, they abandoned the outworks of the war for Zion after conditions improved.

But while they were on the scene, they seemed to some people to be a terrifying political force—all the more so because their arrival coincided with economic collapse. Grover Cleveland and the Democrats had only a brief time to savor their triumph of 1892. The next spring brought a panic followed by the century's worst depression. Hundreds of companies went bankrupt. Unemployment rose to about two and a half million and, in the marvelous new cities of skyscrapers and electric lamps, homeless men lined up for charity soup and a chance to sleep on police-station floors. The irony was sharpest in Chicago, which was then in the midst of a World's Fair to celebrate four hundred triumphant years of American history since Columbus.

Cleveland's second administration was launched in catastrophe, and he was tragically unequipped to respond to it with either compassion or political intelligence. He moved like a battleship (armor-plated in strong convictions), unswervingly through the riptides of depression. He believed that the economy must right itself through the operation of the natural laws of supply and demand. When prices had fallen sufficiently, capital would come out of hiding and wheels would turn once more. (In this view, he resembled another depression President, thirty-seven years later.) But to achieve this end, credit must be kept on a sound basis. The government must maintain the value of the currency by redeeming any of its obligations in gold on demand—greenbacks, Bland-Allison silver dollars, and notes issued in payment for silver purchases under the Sherman Act. This was especially difficult to accomplish in hard times, when there was a tendency to hoard gold, and when the government's revenue from all sources—customs, land sales, and taxes—had declined. The country's gold reserve slumped sharply, and the financial journals that worried about a Treasury surplus in 1890 agonized over a potential gold deficit in 1893.

Cleveland's solution was to demand repeal of the 1890 Silver Purchase Act. He called a special session of Congress, which effected the repeal, but at a heavy political price. Conservative Democrats lined up with hard-money Republicans, while Westerners and Southerners argued that now if ever was the time to throw out the lifeline of currency relief, and damned their own Democratic President as a tool of Wall Street. Ben Tillman dramatized their feelings with his flamboyant threat to "stick my pitchfork" in Cleveland's "fat old ribs." Cleveland further fissured his party by pushing implacably for a revision of the tariff downward to a "revenue-only" basis, despite the inevitable infighting that such a measure would cause. After a debate distinguished for irascibility, the Wilson-Gorman tariff of 1894 emerged with schedules still so high that Cleveland refused to sign it, although it became law without his signature. Its most significant provision was for an income tax, to make up for revenue lost by reductions in some duties, and to make a conciliatory gesture toward deserters to the Populists.

In 1894 there were more frightening events. There was a march of unemployed men on Washington under the leadership of Jacob Coxey. He was an Ohio reformer who proposed that the federal government should inaugurate a program of road-building and other public works, to be paid for in bonds that would circulate as legal tender, thus simultaneously creating jobs and currency. Coxey was eccentrically ahead of his time, and most of his "army" melted away before it reached Washington, where its remnants were arrested, before they could present their petition, for trespassing on the Capitol grounds. But, for a time, he had Americans wondering whether representative government was to be replaced by the "European" revolutionary spectacle of mobs marching on the palace.

Then labor violence broke out afresh. In Chicago, in June of 1894, striking workers in the Pullman-car shops appealed for support to members of a recently organized American Railway Union (ARU), led by Eugene V. Debs. The ARU was a new "industrial" union of all railway workers, challenging the leadership of the "craft" Brotherhoods of engineers, firemen, brakemen, and conductors. Debs, reluctant to test the ARU's strength too far, nevertheless felt compelled to order a boycott of trains that included Pullman cars. The result was a major rail tie-up, accompanied by some violent clashes among police, strikers, and strikebreakers. Cleveland's Attorney General, Richard Olney, helped the railroad owners to secure a federal injunction against the strike. When ARU members ignored the injunction, Olney convinced President Cleveland that the situation was out of hand and demanded federal intervention. This move was bitterly resisted by the Governor of Illinois, a prolabor and pro-Populist Democrat, John P. Altgeld. Nevertheless, Cleveland ordered troops into the city of Chicago in the first week of July, whereupon serious rioting did break out. Ultimately the strike was crushed, but Cleveland had added labor to the growing list of his enemies.

The fall elections of 1894 showed how long that list was. The Democrats suffered an overwhelming defeat—their lead of 90 seats in the House was converted into a Republican majority of 140 seats and, in 24 of the 45 states, they won no Congressional seats at all. There was even greater significance in the fact that the heaviest losses were in the populous Northeast. The traditional loyalty of urban strongholds to the Democrats had been

By the century's end, Eastern farmers were becoming more closely linked to urban markets (hence less attracted to Populism), as shown by this scene of wagons in Washington's Southwest Market, ready to feed the capital city for another day.

shaken. Moreover, the Eastern farmer, even while his Great Plains fellow-agrarian was fleeing to Populism, was staying with the Republicans. Even the Populists lost some ground in the West; while polling a million and a half votes, they lost statewide races to the Republicans in four states that they had carried in 1892—Colorado, Idaho, Kansas, and North Dakota. As compensation, they won sweeping victories in North Carolina and South Carolina. Yet there were signs that 1896 might be a Republican year.

Certainly 1895 further dimmed Cleveland's political future. Still worried about the declining gold reserve, he instructed his Treasury secretary to negotiate several loans of gold from private banking houses, including that of J. P. Morgan. He thus appeared to be going, hat in hand, to beg help from the man who popularly symbolized the arrogance of "the money power" just as Rockefeller embodied, in caricature, the arrogance of the trust. Moreover, in 1895, the Supreme Court rendered two momentous decisions. In the E. C. Knight case, it destroyed much of the potential effectiveness of the Sherman Anti-Trust Act by declaring that a sugar company which dominated the refining industry was exempt from federal antitrust prosecution because the actual manufacture of the sugar took place within the boundaries of a single state. Almost simultaneously, a majority of the justices declared the income-tax provision of the Wilson-Gorman tariff unconstitutional. To thousands of outraged Americans, these two decisions seemed to say the same thing: organized wealth was beyond the reach of federal regulation. To the Populists, these decisions were as sinister as the Dred Scott decision had been to Republicans a generation before, and some men wondered if a civil war between classes was not as inevitable as civil war between sections had been in 1860.

It was against this turbulent background that the 1896 election was fought out with an emotionalism unmatched in the preceding two decades. When the Republicans convened in June, their silver wing was totally outnumbered. The nomination went to William McKinley, an amiable Union veteran, and author of the 1890 tariff, thus identifying the party with "protection" as one of its chief issues. The other issue was provided when the platform supported the gold standard as the cornerstone of prosperity, although McKinley had previously favored international bimetalism, that is, world agreement to peg gold and silver values at a fixed ratio. However, the

As if to emphasize his own rejection of turbulent controversy and his own solid domestic respectability, McKinley did much of his campaigning from the front porch of his Canton, Ohio home. The contrast between this scene and the packed rally for Greeley illustrated on page 117 was not mere chance.

Republican candidate spent little time on the money question, but cam-paigned from his home in Canton, Ohio, as the prospective furnisher of a "full dinner pail" to every American. Prosperity and conciliation were his themes and, although he was upbraided by some people for this apparent vacuity (Vachel Lindsay, the poet, called him "the man without an angle or a tangle"), conciliation may have been what the country really needed that summer.

The Democratic convention was riotous. The majority of delegates, who came prepared to repudiate Cleveland conservatism, found an early test of strength in the vote on the platform. A free-silver plank was proposed and, while it was almost certain to be adopted, a floor debate was scheduled. One of the pro-silver speakers was a thirty-six-year-old former Congressman from Nebraska, William Jennings Bryan. Bryan, born in Illinois in the year of Lincoln's election, had gone to Nebraska as a young lawyer-on-the-make in the best "go West" tradition. He was the last of the Jacksonians—a fundamentalist who believed implicitly that the will of a majority of American commoners was the virtual voice of God, and the final authority in all disputes, whether the subject was money or metaphysics. He distrusted almost everything modern, ranging from the cities and higher criticism of the Bible to "plutocracy," standing armies, and the demon rum. He was a sonorous orator, armed with a vocabulary of symbols—the spirit of '76, the virgin West, the honest yeoman, the sturdy pioneer—which reached deep into the American soul. His speech was a sensation, ending with a powerful appeal to both patriotic and Protestant symbols:

> . . . It is the issue of 1776 over again. Our ancestors, when but three millions in number, had the courage to declare their political independence of every other nation; shall we, their descendants, when we have grown to seventy millions, declare that we are less independent than our forefathers? No, my friends, that will never be the verdict of our people. Therefore, we care not upon what lines the battle is fought. If they say bimetalism is good, but that we cannot have it until other nations help us, we reply that, instead of having a gold standard because England has, we will restore bimetalism and then let England have bimetalism because the United States has it. If they dare to come out in the open field and defend the gold standard as a good thing, we will fight them to the uttermost. Having behind us the producing masses of this nation and the world, supported by the commercial interests, the laboring interests, and the toilers everywhere, we will answer their demand for a gold standard by saying to them: You shall not press down upon the brow of labor this crown of thorns, you shall not crucify mankind upon a cross of gold.

The speech threw the convention into an uproar of approval. The silver men not only carried their point regarding the platform but found in Bryan an appealing if unexpected candidate. He was easily nominated in the afterglow of unrehearsed enthusiasm for his speech.

Bryan's choice by the Democrats created an immediate dilemma for the Populists, who were meeting simultaneously in their convention. Should they concur in the "free silverite" Bryan's nomination, or remain independent? It was an especially hard choice for Southern Populists, who would be asked to cooperate with a Democratic party that they had been reviling for eight years. (As one Southerner put it, the Democratic idea of fusion was that "we play Jonah while they play whale.") But it was also a difficult choice for ideologically dedicated Populists. Bryan was not with them except in temperament and Old Testament figures of speech. He took no public

Political cartoonists—purveyors of a new kind of wit made possible by mass journalism—had a field day with Bryan's youth, wide mouth, and simultaneous nomination by more than one party.

position on the Populist demands other than favoring free silver, and in 1896 would probably have repudiated many of them. Moreover, the Democrats, to placate their own conservatives slightly, gave the Vice-Presidential nomination to Arthur Sewall, a Maine banker and railroad executive. The Populists finally settled on a compromise, endorsing Bryan, but running their own Vice-Presidential nominee, Georgia's Thomas E. Watson.

The campaign was intense. Bryan's refusal to embrace any Populist radicalism outside of free silver was ignored, and conservatives trembled in fear that he would, in one swift stroke as President, devalue the currency, drive every bank in the country into failure, and lay American industry in ruins. "No large political movement in America has ever before spawned such hideous and repulsive vipers," was one typical newspaper view of the Democratic-Populist coalition. And a magazine observed of Bryan: "Probably no man has succeeded in inspiring so much terror without taking life." Marcus A. Hanna, McKinley's campaign manager, shrewdly judged that Bryan was making a mistake in passing over general discontents in favor of the money question (although, to Bryan's eye, unpracticed in complexities, all things would be made new with 16 to 1). "He's talking silver all the time," said Hanna, "and that's where we've got him."

Hanna played on the fears of Republican businessmen in order to build up a massive war chest, and it was widely charged that workingmen were warned that a Bryan victory would mean closed factory gates on the

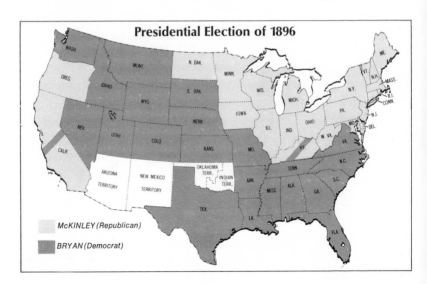

Presidential Election of 1896

McKINLEY (Republican)

BRYAN (Democrat)

day after election. But McKinley's victory was solidly based on more than threats or propaganda. He won 271 votes to Bryan's 176 (with about a 600,000-vote lead in the popular count). Bryan did not carry a single state north of the Ohio River and east of the Mississippi. He won the lower South, but lost West Virginia, Kentucky, Delaware, and Maryland. West of the Mississippi, he lost California, Oregon, Minnesota, North Dakota, and Iowa. Only the cotton South, the silver-mining mountain states, and part of the wheat belt stayed with him.

The verdict of 1896 spelled transition. Wherever industry had rooted itself, the threat (real or imagined) of continued business stagnation as a result of free silver was enough to win votes for McKinley. Not only the laborer but even most farmers outside the depression-wracked wheat and cotton-growing regions identified their futures with open factory doors. The dream of a farmer-labor coalition at the polls to arrest the march of industrial expansion and consolidation—the dream of the Grangers, the Greenback party, and the Knights of Labor—was dead. The Republicans had made a great change of base from the party of the Union and free soil to the party of prosperity and protection. So complete was their victory that after the twenty seesaw political years from 1876 to 1896, they controlled the White House, Senate, and House of Representatives uninterruptedly until 1912.

But it was not a victory for reaction. The party, having pledged itself to an acceptance of industrialism and having received a ratification of that stand, could generate within itself the moral and political momentum to modify industrialism. In the closed ranks behind McKinley (with the exception of a handful of defecting silver Republicans who futilely supported Bryan), there was a security that would allow insurgents and Progressives to challenge and to share in Republican leadership from 1900 to 1912. The Democrats were not to know such internal peace for another political generation.

EPILOGUE: IMPERIALISM AS A FOOTNOTE

The five years following the 1896 election were the climax of an era when the nation encountered the shocks of rapid industrialization. These years wrote farewell to the issues of the 1870s and 1880s. Business began to recover. New gold discoveries in the world eased the money crisis and raised prices enough to move the Northern farmer, at least, into a period of relative prosperity. The Populists faded rapidly and, in 1904, died as a party. Also the Knights of Labor passed from the scene, yielding to the more pragmatic American Federation of Labor. Despite the Sherman Anti-Trust Act, business combinations continued to increase. In 1897 the Republican Congress passed a new tariff act, the highest ever, and followed it shortly afterward with a Gold Standard Act. The tariff remained in force for sixteen years, and the gold standard law continued until 1934. The triumph of protection and sound money and what they stood for was complete.

In the same span of time, by intervening in Cuba and in the Spanish-owned Philippines, America became imperial. Many forces impelled the United States to take this fateful course. There was the traditional American interest in a prospering and cooperative Cuba; there was Social Darwinism, justifying war and expansion as part of the historic mission of the great "Anglo-Saxon" nations; there was the commercial expansionism of the preceding two decades, moving to culmination; there were popular journals that fanned jingoistic passions by luridly describing supposed Spanish atrocities in Cuba; and there was probably an unspoken desire to heal the wounds of 1896 in a common national enterprise. All played a part in bringing us into war in April 1898. A brief land campaign in Cuba, and naval victories in Manila Bay and off Santiago made us victors by July. And these triumphs left the United States with the remnants of the Spanish empire—Cuba, the Philippines, and Puerto Rico. At the outbreak of war the nation had pledged itself, by Congressional resolution, to respect Cuba's independence, but the question of what to do with the other spoils of victory was left open. The McKinley administration finally demanded the Philippines and Puerto Rico and obtained both from Spain in the Treaty of 1899, and the campaign of 1900 was carried on in the shadow of a vigorous discussion as to whether this policy of imperialism was justifiable. Bryan, the Democratic nominee once more, and titular leader of the party, was against annexation, but he confused the question by refusing to urge Democrats in Congress to vote against the treaty. Although the election did not clearly hinge on the issue, the Republican victory could be, and was, interpreted as a mandate for a new policy of exercising American power overseas.

The anti-imperialist debate provides a final footnote on the story of the years from 1877 to 1900. Many of the most outspoken opponents of annexation come from the ranks of intellectuals and reformers who were past fifty, and had been birthright Republicans. They believed that the republic they had known—of equality under law, self-restraint in appetite, and probity in government—would not survive the creation of an empire, complete with military adventurers and swindling proconsuls. But the republic of which they were dreaming had been disappearing for years; 1896 was its funeral rite.

On the other side were the imperialists, many of them vigorous young men, soon to become Progressives. They had reached maturity when the transcontinental railroad, the trust, the city, and the battleship were already realities instead of threatening novelties. They welcomed the power and challenges of the new society. They believed that an empire abroad could coexist with progress at home, and that strong, efficient, modern government could carry out the paternalistic and moralistic goals of the old Protestant tradition. The kind of nation that they dreamed of had been gestating for a long time and, in a sense, the year 1896 was its birth-year.

Perhaps no one typified the view of this younger generation more than Theodore Roosevelt, aged forty-two in 1900. After a brisk political career in the New York state legislature where, despite a vocal support of reform, his political ambitions led him to oppose the Mugwumps, he became successively a Civil Service Commissioner, New York City Police Commissioner, and Assistant Secretary of the Navy. He was made Secretary of the Navy not only because of an interest in naval matters and overseas expansion but because he had prominently campaigned for McKinley and had denounced Bryan in 1896. In 1898 he put on a uniform to help fight the war that he had loudly demanded for so long. He came out of the service to win immediate election to New York's governorship. Older Republican leaders were frightened by the energies of this self-advertised warrior, historian, sportsman, conservationist, cavalryman, journalist, reformer, jingo, and all-around dynamo. They tried to bury him with the Vice-Presidential nomination in 1900.

But history likes its little joke. In the first week of September, 1901, President McKinley—who was fighting the Civil War when "T.R." was a five-year old boy—was shot by an assassin at the Pan-American Exposition in Buffalo, New York. Theodore Roosevelt, a man who enthusiastically embraced the power of the twentieth century with a rhetoric of the nineteenth, became, in a rare coincidental meeting of the man and the hour, the first true American president of that century. A new age had begun.

Chapter VIII

Changing Historical Literature of an Age of Change

In formal historical writing, Americans have long and perhaps unwittingly viewed the last twenty-five years of the nineteenth century through the lenses of emotional involvement. As we have seen, while the United States grew in wealth and power during those years, her citizens were alternately elated and troubled by their historical experience. There was, on the one hand, a glow of pride; yet, on the other, a deep uneasiness over the threat to basic American values and institutions posed by such growth. This tension was reflected in almost all of the social and political conflicts of the 1890s, and it endured into the Progressive era of 1900 to 1917. Historians who matured during this period of nearly three decades showed the effects of the prevailing intellectual dilemma. Nowhere is this more visible than in the writings of the three giants whose influence was vastly pervasive in American historical letters until the 1930s and 1940s: Frederick Jackson Turner, Vernon L. Parrington, and Charles A. Beard. Their views furnished the starting point for innumerable explorations of the 1875 to 1900 era, and the underlying motif of much writing on that period, since about 1950, has been a change in the focus that they provided.

Turner was an actor in the drama at the close of the nineteenth century. His paper, "The Significance of the Frontier in American History," delivered to the then-youthful American Historical Association in 1893, was one more expression of the underlying uneasiness about the direction of "progress" that was the obverse of the coin of Social Darwinism. Turner argued that the disappearance of an unlimited area of free land contiguous to the settled United States spelled the end of an era in American life. He dated this disappearance from about 1890, which was essentially premature, since much of the Far West was still unsettled in 1900, and the greatest single year for original entries under the Homestead Act was 1910. However, the significance of Turner's essay was in its unspoken question which, to him and to many in his generation, was far from premature: What would replace the frontier? If the dynamic and democratic forces in American life had gained new strength every time they touched a new area of virgin land, then could the United States mobilize these liberating energies when the open continent was closed? Would freedom and individualism then vanish? Nearly sixty years later, a follower of Turner, Walter Prescott Webb, suggested as much for the Western world as a whole. In *The Great Frontier,*[1] Webb wondered if the whole European-American democratic ideology could survive the exhaustion of the riches in land and resources opened by the discovery of the New World about four and a half centuries ago.

Turner appeared reluctant to pursue such a line of inquiry to stark conclusions. He turned his remarkable gifts as an historian away from the period in which he lived, and devoted himself, instead, to a life-long study of the West before 1850. Few historians of that generation concerned themselves with "recent" times, which they regarded as being outside the scope of "correct" historical inquiry, but it may be that Turner avoided the immediate past partly because he was reluctant to face the future.

Vernon L. Parrington's place in American historical letters is unique. Essentially a student of "literature," he embraced in that category an enormous range of polemical political writings, and his three-volume work, *Main Currents in American Thought* became a compendium of American history seen through the eyes of almost every major figure who committed himself to print, whether in a seventeenth-century sermon or a nineteenth-century pamphlet on the tariff. Parrington, who was in spirit a flaming amalgam of populist, progressive, and socialist, viewed all American history as a war between the democratic aspirations of the many (especially farmers, debtors, laborers, and radical thinkers) and the few (notably merchants, manufacturers, bankers, speculators, and their conservative political and theological defenders). The writers whom he did not herd ruthlessly into one of the two camps, he dismissed as "romantics." But *Main Currents* was brilliantly written and became a virtual Bible for a generation of young historians. In the graduate schools of the 1930s and 1940s, everyone who

---

[1] Walter P. Webb. *The Great Frontier,* 1952.

hoped to discourse intelligently on the American past read it, and argued with and from it, usually with pleasure.

Therefore, Parrington's views on the post-Civil War era would be of special consequence in framing the outlook of historians, but he never fully developed his interpretation, since he died while writing his third volume (beginning in 1865) and left only skeleton notes for most of it. But, from these, and from his crackling opening chapters on Grant's America, he clearly regarded the post-Appomattox years as vulgar and insensitive, deserving his arresting label, "The Great Barbecue." For all his liberalism, he recognized that the rush to get rich had won the sanction of Jacksonians fully as well as Whigs. He began, then, to analyze the protest literature of the 1880s and 1890s as an effort to expose the moral contradictions of an acquisitive *and* democratic society. Significantly, the title he picked for the last third of his study was "The Beginnings of Critical Realism."

Of this trio of historical writers, only Charles Beard wrote directly and fully about the three decades preceding 1900. Like Turner and Parrington, Beard was nurtured in the atmosphere of Midwestern progressivism and, for him even more than for them, the driving forces of political life were economic (a lesson he learned not so much from Karl Marx as from *The Federalist.*) The central fact of the early nineteenth century, he asserted, had been a clash between contending types of capital, in which each side developed a political philosophy appropriate to its needs. One type, represented by the Southern planter, was agrarian and centered in the ownership and control of land and natural resources; the other, represented by Northern businessmen, was mercantile and manufacturing-oriented; both were expansionistic. The Civil War was thus a "Second American Revolution" in which men whose power was drawn from mercantile and manufacturing capital won control of the national government, made it supreme, and used it to burst through the barriers that "strict construction" had placed in the way of their drive for power. Beard spelled out this theme in his influential textbook of 1927, *The Rise of American Civilization,* written in collaboration with his wife. Into this context of the triumph of industrial, financial, and mercantile captialism, he fitted most of the intellectual, social, and political developments of 1865 to 1898. The ambitions of "business" resumed specie payments, carved up the public domain among exploiters, set commercial outposts in the Pacific, reared the cities, worked revolutions in manufacturing and agriculture whose fruits were generally denied to the worker and the farmer, and finally coerced endorsement from the electorate in 1896.

What stands out in these three interpretations is, first, the force and vitality of what might be called a Mugwump-like distrust of modernity itself, or at least a Progressive concern over the "excesses" of modernity. None of the historians mentioned can be described as a celebrant of industrial growth and power. It was left to the Andrew Carnegies, the Russell Conwells, and the popular biographers of the early twentieth century to sing the glories of the captains of industry and the imperial nation. However, even among writers for the general public, there were sour notes; in 1909, Gustavus Myers' *History of the Great American Fortunes* cast a very cold eye on the process by which many of the nation's leading business dynasties had accumulated their wealth and power, and twenty-five years later, Matthew Josephson's *The Robber Barons,*[2] a work in much the same spirit, was widely influential. The major professional historians, meanwhile, tended to confine themselves to the colonial and "middle" periods of American history, leaving the "modern" field untilled.

A second conspicuous feature of the tradition of Turner, Parrington, and Beard was its emphasis on conflicts in the American past—conflicts between East and West, frontier and settlement, pioneer and speculator, merchant and planter, protectionist and free-trader, lender and borrower, and worker and employer. This outlook, too, bore the stamp of the Populist-Progressive generation that refracted American political life through these conflicts, and tried to mediate or resolve them. The outlook had its analytical and stylistic virtues, but it also had some clear limitations. Among them was a tendency to fit issues into a Procrustean bed. Many questions were slighted. Among them were questions such as race and immigration (except where immigration impinged on labor policy), the growth in the scope and organization of government, the changing social styles of classes and masses, the economic impact of technological and entrepreneurial forces on industrial expansion, the pressure of new ideas on the perceptions and imaginitions of nativist and radical, hayseed and urbanite, fundamentalist Christian and "social gospeller." In picturing a society divided into two camps defined by economic interest, historians of the Populist-Progressive school failed to probe deeply into the basic texture, the warp and woof, the patterns of relationship woven through that society.

Any survey of American historical writing in recent years must necessarily take into account that the tradition of Turner, Parrington, and Beard,

---

[2] Matthew Josephson. *The Robber Barons: The Great American Capitalists, 1861–1901,* 1934.

previously outlined, has been undergoing steady erosion. Present-day historians are examining American values with a new detachment from the emotions
of the past. They are, with rare exceptions, uninvolved in the passions of
Populism, civil service reform, or immigration restriction. They do not vote
against the municipal boss, or in favor of free trade, or for the eight-hour
day. Currently, they are more likely to suggest what the proponents of these
panaceas had in common with their enemies than to take sides by implication.
It has, been argued that there is in progress a search for "consensus" in
the American past, which has softened ideological conflicts too generously,
has undervalued our radicalisms, and has painted the landscape in the moral
gray of value-neutralism. A book that seems to illustrate this tendency is
Louis Hartz's *The Liberal Tradition in America*.[3] In it, the author stresses
the absence of genuine conservatism in American thought and the almost
universal faith among all classes in progress, individualism, and nationalism.
Daniel J. Boorstin's *The Genius of American Politics*[4] explicitly hails the
freedom of American political life from ideology; and other works could
be cited that also stress what Americans have held in common, rather than
what they have debated. But this argument among persons who seek out
consensus and persons who expose conflict in the historical record is not
always a disagreement between the committed and the dispassionate scholar.
The historian who finds common ground between traditional antagonists
of the Gilded Age is often rendering an unspoken moral verdict on the
essential materialism, parochialism, or lack of sophistication of all parties.

Moreover, what appears to be a stress on consensus is often an effort
to seek more complex historical groupings than are confined within the
simple polarities of a Parrington. History as a discipline has undergone
evolution. It no longer hopes, as formerly, to establish general laws,
sequences, and overall explanations of human behavior. While Turner and
his disciples, in fact, eventually refined their studies away from a simple
monistic interpretation which held, for example, that democracy was "the
product" of the frontier, nonetheless at root they continued to account for
a great many diverse phenomena—ranging from universal suffrage and revivals
to pet banks—by citing the frontier's influence. And Beard, in his attempt
to find a synthesizing principle in the effect of economic forces on political

---

[3] Louis Hartz. *The Liberal Tradition in America; An Imterpretation of American Political
Thought Since the Revolution*, 1955.

[4] Daniel J. Boorstin. *The Genius of American Politics*, 1953.

life sometimes dealt almost casually with noneconomic phenomena. He paid little attention, for example, to the moral or social implications of the conflict over slavery, since he considered it as merely a vehicle for the political warfare of planters and merchant-manufacturers. Today's historians are more likely to seek out many interrelated patterns and forces behind events, none of which are clearly difinable as "causes." In this way they tend to follow the example of the modern social sciences.

If we examine a series of recent contributions to the study of industrialism—the money question, imperialism, labor, the farmer, and Populism—this regard for the complexity of history will become clearer. We may begin with the consideration of a fresh approach to the history of business, dating from the 1940s and 1950s, which broke away from the pattern of condemnation of business leaders' aggrandizement in favor of a consideration of industrial problems as management saw them. Studies in this mold were not necessarily intended to rehabilitate the "robber barons," although Allan Nevins' two-volume biography of John D. Rockefeller[5] (originally written in 1940 and updated in 1953), seemed to glorify the oil magnate by giving credit to his organizing talents, far-ranging perception of marketing and productive possibilities, and heroic scale of operations. But writers on corporate development, such as Ralph and Muriel Hidy in their 1955 study of Standard Oil of New Jersey,[6] or Thomas Cochran in his 1948 history of the Pabst Brewing Company,[7] or any of the numerous authors who did volumes in "entrepreneurial history" under the aegis of the Harvard Business School, were not interested in praising industrialists any more than in blaming them. They asked new and intriguing questions. What was the actual contribution of each of the many factors in industrial growth? How much credit did the "captains of industry" actually deserve for foresight and planning? How much credit should be allotted to other elements such as the availability of labor, the tariff, the pace of invention, or the social readiness of the marketplace for certain kinds of consumer goods? What, in short, were the actual components of a "system" of "big

---

[5] Allan Nevins. *Study in Power: John D. Rockefeller, Industrialist and Philanthropist*, 1953. 2 v.

[6] Ralph W. and Muriel E. Hidy. *Pioneering in Big Business, 1882–1911: History of Standard Oil (New Jersey)*, 1955.

[7] Thomas C. Cochran. *The Pabst Brewing Company: the History of an American Business*, 1948.

business," and how did they fit together? These questions moved away from the Progressive concern with ethics and intentions of businessmen, and toward a reworking of older categories.

This trend, begun by entrepreneurial studies, has continued and has displayed itself recently in a new kind of economic history: a history that is more sophisticatedly statistical than its predecessors, and is less hospitable not only to the moral judgments but to the periodization of the political historians. In 1961 there appeared Douglass North's *The Economic Growth of the United States, 1790–1860*,[8] in which he presented evidence strongly suggesting that the industrial growth of the United States did not begin with the Civil War era (as was long assumed), but was in flower by the late 1850s. Considering the development of internal and foreign commerce, the size of the labor force, the magnitude of the investment in manufacturing, and the percentage of total resources diverted to it and to the creation of a modern transportation system, and other similar factors, it seemed that we had already completed, in W.W. Rostow's metaphor, our industrial take-off. Thomas C. Cochran argued further, in a significant article of 1961[9] (which was sharply challenged)[10] that the Civil War did not even stimulate an ongoing process of industrial growth, but retarded it by diverting basic resources into war's waste.

The significance of these contributions is twofold. They show, first, what can be done by an analysis of the economy as a functioning mechanism without reference to what people believe is happening—for, certainly, few men in 1860 thought of the United States as a nation that had already completed the transition to an industrially based order. Would it shed new light on a period to find that men were behaving as if they lived in one kind of world, when they were in fact already part of another? Does a historical "era" actually begin until people are aware of it? The whole nature of the historian's enterprise is opened to new evaluation by an economic history like that of North, based on a statistical "reality" not always consonant with political and social "reality" as the men of a given day saw it—the kind that historical documentation has customarily dealt with.

---

[8] Douglass C. North. *The Economic Growth of the U.S., 1790–1860*, 1961.

[9] Thomas C. Cochran. "Did the Civil War Retard Industrialization?" *Mississippi Valley Historical Review*, 51, (1964–5).

[10] Pershing Vartanian. "The Cochran Thesis: A Critique in Statistical Analysis," *Mississippi Valley Historical Review*, 51 (1964–65.)

Second, to put industrialization as a force in national life back into the 1840s rather than the 1860s is to alter seriously the notion that the Civil War made the industrial surge politically possible. It would seem more justifiable to say the reverse: that political alignments followed new lines or force created by an already-ripening industrialism itself. This statement would support Beard's argument concerning the strength of economic "gravitation" on political "apples," but it would change other portions of his thesis. Instead of a conscious business class planning industrial growth and shaping political policy to its ends, we now see a variety of men of business, united in the desire to take advantage of expansion, but responding to an ever-changing economic setting by many different kinds of political behavior, changing frequently as need suggested.

This is the picture sketched in a number of recent works on business attitudes toward post-Civil War questions. Stanley Coben examined the views of businessmen on Reconstruction in 1959.[11] His research was based on trade and commercial journals and other similar sources from 1866 to 1877. To be consistent with the Beardian scheme, these publications should have consistently favored a Radical "hard line" toward the South in order to keep the planter class disfranchised and immobile. But the editorial spokesmen for business disagreed as widely among themselves as they did with any other indentifiable economic group on the policies that ought to be followed. Simultaneously with Coben's article, there appeared Robert P. Sharkey's *Money, Class, and Party*,[12] which contradicted Coben's article in one sense and reinforced it in another. In comparing the attitudes of a number of men of affairs toward Reconstruction with their attitudes toward inflation, Sharkey emerged with a conclusion that was satisfactory to economic determinism: the economic orientation of every group studied was a major element in defining its political program. But Sharkey also indicated that men's needs in the economic realm were preceived in many different ways, as Coben also demonstrated. What determined a man's feelings both about greenbacks *and* whether to withdraw troops from the South was his sense of how these decisions would impinge on his livelihood. However, his method of making a living, although important to his outlook, could not

[11] Stanley Coben. "Northern Businessmen and Radical Reconstruction: A Re-Examination," *Mississippi Valley Historical Review*, 46 (1959–60).

[12] Robert Sharkey. *Money, Class and Party: An Economic Study of Civil War and Reconstruction*, 1959.

be defined simply as "business" or "agriculture" but as a particular kind of business at a particular time and place. There is the key. To talk of "men of business" is to talk of large manufacturere, small shopowners, textile makers, iron masters, railroad builders—an infinite list of men drawn from every sectional and political background. Also "the farmer" was as varied as the crops, soils, agricultural markets and resources, and systems of land tenure in the United States. Thus to talk of "the triumph of capitalism" or "the business classes" instead of "the triumph of Radicalism" or "the North" is simply to substitute one large order of generalization for another.

This conclusion is ratified in Irwin Unger's 1964 work, *The Greenback Era*,[13] which indicates complex and shifting connections among bondholders, resumptionists, state-bank men, national-bank men, greenbackers, silverites, and others—coalitions that the terms "hard-money men" and "soft-money men" barely define. Unger, in this way, is challenging a tendency of earlier historians to superimpose the conflicts of 1896 (involving Republican support for gold and Democratic support for silver) on the era of Reconstruction.

The same mosaic of interests is revealed by other studies of class and economic conflict. In one sense, C. Vann Woodward's *Origins of the New South*[14] develops a motif implicit in both Beard and Turner; that is, that the South, like the West, was exploited by the national fiscal power consolidated in the Northeast. Yet Woodward shows clearly that the "business mentality" was not absent from the former Confederacy, and that the South generated its own set of adherents to the virtues of the railroad and the factory. Southern businessmen were quite willing to invite the development of their region's resources by Northern capital, even when the process involved the subordination of other Southern needs.

In fact, the tradition that speaks of "businessmen" as if they were a wholly coherent group of identical thinkers is giving way to a tradition that does not attempt to rehabilitate "robber barons" as much as it attempts to reconstruct the pathways between their many varieties of economic and social thought. One book that undertakes this task is Edward C. Kirkland's *Dream and Thought in the American Business Community*.[15] In assessing the feelings, as revealed in correspondence, of certain presumably representative business

---

[13] Irwin Unger. *The Greenback Era: a Social and Political History of American Finance, 1865–1879,* 1964.

[14] C. Vann Woodward. *Origins of the New South, 1877–1913,* 1951.

[15] Edward C. Kirkland. *Dream and Thought in the American Business Community, 1860–1900,* 1964.

leaders, Kirkland finds them less uniformly devoted to a crude, oversimplified Social Darwinism than was indicated by an earlier study such as Richard Hofstadter's 1944 work, *Social Darwinism in American Thought*.[16] Indeed, a "businessman's" attitudes were the result of the pushes and pulls of many inherited traditions and expectations in his entire life style. If his work in the office was the core of that style, it was nevertheless not all of it.

It was also a part of the Beardian tradition that market-hungry businessmen supported and sustained imperial expansion. Temporarily out of favor, this thesis now reemerges, with modifications, in the work of William Appleman Williams and in the work of one of his students, Walter LaFeber. In *The New Empire*.[17] LaFeber reasserts that the search for markets and investment opportunities was an underlying theme in the diplomacy of all our Secretaries of State from William H. Seward to the end of the century. But LaFeber contends that the yearning for foreign customers and resources was significantly not confined to "capitalists." By 1898 the farmer was convinced (as he had often been, whether or not the facts warranted the belief) that he must have overseas markets or be buried in his surpluses. The rationalizations of Josiah Strong, Alfred Thayer Mahan, and other prophets of empire were not merely echoes of the wishes of a definable "business class," but were expressions of a general outlook spread indistinguishably among many parties and factions. Many businessmen were anti-imperialists before 1898, preferring the commercial conquest of far-off lands (or, more likely home markets) to grim-visaged war with its unpredictable effects on the business cycle and its high taxes. For Americans of every sort, life was a matter of business, and this viewpoint was reflected in national policy. And this is not the precise impression that Beard intended to convey.

A recent essay by Herbert Gutman opens a new approach to the study of late nineteenth century labor history.[18] Gutman maintains that it is a mistake to read the aspirations of "labor" through the prism of union spokesmanship, since at this time only a small proportion of the labor force was unionized. Also, it is erroneous to view the labor record as one of constant frustration imposed by hostile capitalists and their spokesmen. In fact, the relations between labor and capital were complex and diffuse. In

[16] Richard Hofstadter. *Social Darwinism in American Thought, 1860–1915,* 1944.

[17] Walter La Feber. *The New Empire; An Interpretation of American Expansion, 1860–1898,* 1963.

[18] Gutman, Herbert. "The Worker's Search for Power." *The Gilded Age: A Reappraisal.* ed. by H. Wayne Morgan, 1963.

the smaller towns of the nation, the lines between workmen and the middle-class community were less visible, social conscience played a role in mitigating conflict, and economic classes tended to merge in common centers of life and residence.

We must be wary of assuming that the central tendency of modern scholarship is to blend and melt all Americans into an indefinable class of fellow-believers in the same shibboleths, or to soften the sharpness of the conflicts that erupted. The point is, instead, that in the interaction between changes wrought by industrialism, on one hand, and long-held American values of egalitarianism and Christian conscience, on the other, many positions were developed from a wide diversity of starting points. The categorizations are far from simple. If we say "urban," do we refer to large or small cities? If we say "Protestant," of what denomination do we speak? If we talk of the laborer, do we refer to a skilled or an unskilled worker, in a growing industry or a declining one, concentrated or diffused among small owners, with many geographical centers or a few? If we refer to the immigrant, do we mean the recent arrival or the veteran of twenty years' Americanization? These questions, ruthlessly pursued, can be dangerous. They can ultimately destroy any generalization, and to some degree, and warily, historians must generalize. Yet the problem poses an exciting challenge to contemporary historians. It is to make a picture out of different-colored and many-sized fragments, to find drama not in the foreordained march of forces, but in contingent and uncertain choices of living men.

A final area in which this challenge is being accepted is in the study of the election of 1896 and its background, long a battlefield of contending generalizations. A number of new works have appeared which circumscribe a lively controversy: How should we characterize the Populists and their foes? In 1955, in *The Age of Reform,*[19] Richard Hofstadter fired an opening gun. His initial chapters disputed the theory that Populism was a movement of the virtuous but exploited yeoman against the forces of oppression. He denied that Populism had furnished the basic impetus to the reform movement, which later flowered in Progressivism. He also denied, indeed, that the "happy yeoman" had existed at all as a soil-rooted countryman, sturdily exemplifying an anti-industrial way of life.

Instead, the American farmer had always been a small capitalist seeking to maximize the return on his investment, and he exhibited all the fears,

---

[19] Richard Hofstadter. *The Age of Reform: from Bryan to F.D.R.,* 1955.

suspicions, and anxieties of that class. His debts were generally incurred in the purchase of land beyond his immediate needs, which he hoped, in many cases, to hold for speculative gain (a point partly confirmed by Allan Bouge's study of farm mortgages in Iowa),[20] or in the purchase of equipment designed to raise his cash income. Hofstadter further contended that in the revivalistic rhetoric of Populism, the high-plains farmer revealed certain unadmirable secrets of his being. He denounced Wall Street and the Eastern moneyed interests. Was this not a forerunner of the kind of devil theory that could later be translated into hysterical anti-Communism? He denounced the evils of the city. Was not this a kind of xenophobia irritated into frenzy by the urban presence of large numbers of immigrants? He denounced the Rothschilds and the English, whose banking practices were the support of the gold standard. Was not this a portent of anti-Semitism and isolationism? In short, Hofstadter wondered whether a line could be drawn from Populism, through the Ku Klux Klan of the 1920s, and the isolationism of the 1930s, and to the McCarthyism of the 1950s—all movements with certain similarities in rhetoric and with headquarters in the "American Gothic" midwest.

The response to Hofstadter, and to others who shared his views, has forced historians to modify their traditional view of 1896 as a clash of antogonistic worlds. C. Vann Woodward, writing from the vantage point of a mastery of Southern Populism (which Hofstadter's analysis had ignored) warned that it was dangerous to abstract the rhetoric of a movement from its economic roots, a reminder that there was some virtue in the Beardian viewpoint.[21] The Populists, after all, had genuine economic grievances, and they behaved as we might have expected Americans to behave whose future seemed hopeless. They were in the grain of American political protest. Walter T. K. Nugent quarried the source material of Kansas Populism and showed that the movement in that state was a temporary coalition of hard-pressed middle-class farmers indistinguishable from their neighbors in all but their financial plight, who, regardless of popular diatribes against the Rothschilds uttered in the heat of campaigns, were quite willing to accept votes and support from any group that offered them, including foreigners and Jews.[22]

---

[20] Allan Bogue. *Money at Interest: Farm Mortgages on the Middle Border*, 1955.

[21] C. Vann Woodward. "The Populist Heritage and the Intellectual," *American Scholar,* 29, (1959–60).

[22] Walter T. K. Nugent. *The Tolerant Populists: Kansas, Populism and Nativism*, 1963.

Thus, Populism became less of a holy crusade and more of a "traditional" third-party protest. However, Norman Pollack, in *The Populist Response to Industrial America*[23] (1962), reinvoked the emotional climate of 1896 by insisting that the Populists had, indeed, laid their finger on the ills of a society where wealth accumulated and men decayed, and had been in spirit if not in specific legislative accomplishment the forerunners of the contemporary drive for social betterment. But almost simultaneously, J. Rogers Hollingsworth's *The Whirligig of Politics*[24] explained Populism's rise partially in terms of the inability of the Democratic party to deal constructively with the discontents of the West and the South, so that the Republican victory of 1896 was due as much to a major party's temporary failure to adjust to a situation as to anything else. It was, in short, a significant but not abnormal political event. Hollingsworth, Nugent, and Woodward thus countered Hofstadter not by defending the Populist ideology, as Pollack had tended to do, but rather by focusing on the nonideological behavior of the People's Party.

Following a long generation dominated by historians writing in the frame of reference set by Turner, Parrington, and Beard, a time seems at hand when modern scholars find it possible to study the years from 1877 to 1901 without becoming, even unintentionally, partisans in the very issues they seek to define. They do not self-consciously seek to argue for "progress" or to condemn those who appeared to stand in its way. These new historians cast cool glances at the slogans of conservatism and progressivism alike. Their primary loyalty is to their craft and its national academic fraternity. They gladly seek liaison with other disciplines and, in those disciplines as well as their own, are finding patterns distinct from those of their predecessors. Perhaps this change is the most significant element in all of the recent writings that embrace the data, as well as the perceptions, of the great age of change from the end of Reconstruction to the end of the century.

[23] Norman Pollack. *The Populist Response to Industrial America; Midwestern Populist Thought,* 1962.

[24] J. Rogers Hollingsworth. *The Whirligig of Politics; the Democracy of Cleveland and Bryan,* 1963.

Illustration Credits

Page 14: Collections of the Library of Congress. Page 15: top, Historical Pictures Service—Chicago; bottom, Historical Pictures Service—Chicago. Page 36: Collections of the Library of Congress. Page 41: Courtesy of the Chicago Historical Society. Page 46: Courtesy of the Moody Bible Institute. Page 56: Collections of the Library of Congress (from the George Eastman House Collection, E. P. Vollum Collection of Gold Rush Photographs). Page 58: Courtesy of the Remington Art Memorial, Ogdensburg, New York. Page 59: Courtesy of the Kansas State Historical Society, Topeka. Page 65: top, Historical Pictures Service—Chicago; bottom, Collections of the Library of Congress. Page 74: Collections of the Library of Congress. Page 78: Collections of the Library of Congress, photo by Jacob A. Riis. Page 79: Courtesy of the Nebraska State Historical Society, S. D. Butcher Collection. Page 82: Courtesy of the State Historical Society of Wisconsin, International Harvester Collection. Page 90: Courtesy of the George Eastman House Collection, photo by Lewis W. Hine. Page 98: Copyright Radio Times Hulton Picture Library. Page 105: Courtesy of the Chicago Historical Society. Page 106: top, Courtesy of The Preservation Society of Newport County, Newport, Rhode Island; bottom, Collections of the Library of Congress. Page 107: Courtesy of the Jefferson Medical College of Philadelphia, photographed by the Philadelphia Museum of Art. Page 108: Courtesy of the Chicago Historical Society, photo by Falk. Page 117: Historical Pictures Service—Chicago. Page 130: Collections of the Library of Congress. Page 131: Courtesy of the Smithsonian Institution, Division of Political History. Page 133: Collections of the Library of Congress.

Index

153